THE SHEPHERD LEADER

By Jim VanYperen

ChurchSmart
RESOURCES

St. Charles IL 60174
1-800-253-4276

The Shepherd Leader created by Jim Van Yperen, Executive Director, Metanoia Ministries

This edition of *The Shepherd Leader* has been prepared as companion to the curriculum published by ChurchSmart Resources, Inc.
Strategic Leadership Formation is a comprehensive curriculum combining principles of spiritual formation with leadership development into one, powerful resource.

For more information contact: Jim Van Yperen, Box 448 Washington, NH 03280 603.495.0035 www.changeyourmind.net

All scripture quotations are from the New International Version of the Holy Bible © 1984 International Bible Society, Zondervan Publishers

Published by ChurchSmart Resources

We are an evangelical Christian publisher committed to producing excellent products at affordable prices to help church leaders accomplish effective ministry in the areas of Church planting, Church growth, Church renewal and Leadership development.

For a free catalog of our resources call 1-800-253-4276.

Cover design: Julie Becker

THE SHEPHERD LEADER

Dedication

With love and gratitude to my wife Sharon,
and our children Nate and Sarah.

Savior like a Shepherd Lead Us

Savior like a shepherd lead us,
Much we need Thy tender care;
In Thy pleasant pastures feed us,
For our use Thy folds prepare:
Blessed Jesus, blessed Jesus,
Thou has bought us, Thine we are
Blessed Jesus, blessed Jesus,
Thou has bought us, Thine we are

We are Thine; do Thou befriend us,
Be the Guardian of our way;
Keep Thy flock, from sin defend us,
Seek us when we go astray
Blessed Jesus, blessed Jesus,
Hear, O hear us when we pray,
Blessed Jesus, blessed Jesus,
Hear, O hear us when we pray.

Thou hast promised to receive us,
Poor and sinful though we be;
Thou has mercy to relieve us,
Grace to cleanse, and powír to free;
Blessed Jesus, blessed Jesus,
Early, let us turn to Thee
Blessed Jesus, blessed Jesus,
Early, let us turn to Thee.

Early let us seek Thy favor
Early let us do Thy will;
Blessed Lord and only Savior,
With Thy love our bosoms fill:
Blessed Jesus, blessed Jesus,
Thou has loved us, love us still,
Blessed Jesus, blessed Jesus,
Thou hast loved us, love us still.

– attributed to Dorothy A. Thrupp

Table of Contents

Introduction

The LORD is my shepherd, I shall not be in want. Psalm. 23:1

It was a cold mid-February morning years ago when something happened on our small sheep farm that has become a kind of parable to me for the church today. The night was relatively warm, the temperature hovering around freezing. Most of my Dorset ewes had already lambed and I knew that Elizabeth, my prize ewe, was due to give birth any day. Milk was filling her udders. She was growing restless, pawing the ground and lying down away from the other sheep – a sign that lambing was near.

Normally, when a ewe is about to lamb, I enclose her in a small lambing pen, a rectangular area inside the barn. This gives the ewe a private, clean space to give birth and a shelter to protect the newborn lamb from cold winds or being stepped on by the other sheep. I didn't pen Elizabeth in on this night. I didn't check in on her every two hours, as a good shepherd would.

During the night, the north wind picked up, bringing with it wet snow and a sudden drop in temperature, well below freezing. Early that morning, Elizabeth started labor. Lambs are remarkably resistant to cold weather. I've had ewes lamb in temperatures far below freezing. The lambs will be fine as long as the mother tends to the lamb right away and the newborn is sheltered from the wind. Elizabeth had given us twins for three years running. She was a good mother.

This night was different. Early the next morning I awoke and went out to the barn for morning chores. The moment I saw Elizabeth in the paddock, I knew something was wrong. There were signs of afterbirth but no lambs. Usually, a lamb will huddle close to the mother's side, or bleat loudly trying to find her. There was no lamb in sight, no bleating to be heard.

Searching the barn first, then outside in the paddock, my eye caught the outline of a lamb, lying motionless on the ground, snow-covered. I rushed over, picked the frozen lamb up in my arms and ran to the house, calling my wife Sharon to help. Immediately we began rubbing the stomach and sides of the lamb warming the frozen body in front of our wood stove.

Suddenly it occurred to me. Elizabeth usually had twins. Had there been two lambs outside and I missed one? I rushed back outside to the paddock. There, lying under a thin blanket of snow not far from where I found the first lamb, was not one but two more lambs, both frozen. Elizabeth had had triplets.

I scooped up the two lambs and raced back inside. By now our children, Nate and Sarah, were awake. Giving one lamb to each we spent the next half-hour trying to coax some life into those lambs.

The lambs felt warmer and every once in awhile our hopes would lift as it appeared one was breathing. But it was a false hope. A few minutes more and we knew it was no use. We could not save them. All three lambs were dead.

We laid the lambs down on the towels in front of the stove and looked at them, really seeing them for the first time. They were three, good size, beautifully white, spotless lambs, two females and a male.

They looked perfect, but they were dead.

This happened on our small farm years ago, but it is a parable for my life and for church leadership today. As I looked down on those lambs I thought about my failure. For years, I wanted to tend sheep. I liked calling myself a shepherd. But losing those lambs taught me a lesson – having sheep does not make one a shepherd, any more than having a church makes one a leader.

Many talk and write about leadership. Yet, for all our efforts to resuscitate our egos and polish our methods, we risk becoming leaders and building churches that appear outwardly successful but are frozen dead on the inside. In the end, a church is a reflection of, and will never rise above, the character of its leaders.

This short book is about shepherding and about leadership. Specifically, we will explore and describe the character and competency of a spiritual leader – what we will call a Shepherd Leader.

I write this having lived and learned in two worlds. For ten years I raised sheep on a small farm in New Hampshire. For most of my life I have served in various leadership roles in the marketplace and in the church.

When these worlds merged many years ago, I was struck by how caring for sheep was teaching me vital lessons about leading people. I noticed principles in Scripture that I had always taken for granted.

For instance, I noticed that most biblical leaders were shepherds before they became spiritual leaders. Nearly every Old Testament leader was a shepherd first. Sheep and shepherding are images that Scripture uses frequently, sometimes exclusively, to describe God's people, His purpose, and those He calls to lead. Jesus, for example, refers to himself as both sheep and shepherd. Spiritual leaders are called "shepherds" in both testaments.

I wondered, what was it about shepherding that prepared or equipped a leader to lead? Was it coincidental or does the description have purpose, even profound meaning, that could help our understanding about leadership today?

Answering this question led me to a deeper study of Scripture. I looked up all the references for sheep and shepherd. To understand what the original hearers of Scripture understood about shepherding, I then turned to researching ancient Near Eastern shepherding customs and practices. As we began serving dozens of churches in conflict, I noticed how leadership failure and specifically a lack of biblical shepherding was often at the root of the conflict.

All this has led me to the conclusion that there is a reciprocal relationship between shepherding and leading. First, shepherding is vital for what it teaches the shepherd; or what happens in the leader. Shepherding forms character in the leader; it shapes a certain way of seeing, thinking about and practicing leadership. But second, shepherding is vital for describing a certain kind of people. Shepherding creates a community that shapes a people. This happens through a leader. Shepherding is about: in then through, character then community, and how each shapes the other.

If this conclusion is true, then most books on leadership miss the critical point.

Leadership cannot be measured by the performance of the leader, but by the fruit of those who follow. Success cannot be tallied by the attraction of a crowd, but by persevering faith in the face of suffering or persecution. This begs the question to all leaders: "What kind of followers are you forming?"

Shepherding forces us to change our mind about how we understand leadership, and about how we equip those who lead. This book is about my change of mind: the discovery that leadership is not about leaders, but followers; and that spiritual shepherding always points to Christ, never to the leader.

To lead, one must first hear and follow the voice of Christ, the Great Shepherd of the sheep; then describe what it would look like, and invite others to do the same.

SECTION ONE:
Why Shepherding

He tends his flock like a shepherd: He gathers the lambs
in his arms and carries them close to his heart;
he gently leads those that have young. Isaiah 40:11

Of all the leadership models in Scripture – prophet, priest, king, or judge – God exhorts spiritual leaders to be shepherds. Why? Why does Jesus say to Peter, "feed my sheep?" Why does Paul commend the Ephesian elders to "keep watch" and to "be shepherds?" Why does God choose a shepherd to describe the role of a church leader? Why not a teacher, or priest, or prophet or some other good office? Why, when prophets and priests fail in the Old Testament, does God rebuke them as shepherds?

One obvious explanation is the context and culture of the biblical narrative. The life of a shepherd was common, and easily understood in Near Eastern culture. Certainly every reader of the Old and New Testaments had ready knowledge and experience of both sheep and shepherds. They could merely look up to the hillside and see sheep and shepherds.

But the role of teacher and priest was also common. Why not call leaders to be priests or teachers? If leading a worship service or preparing an expositional sermon was the highest, most important role for a leader, as some suggest, we would expect for Jesus to have said so, or done so. Yet Jesus rarely preached or led worship. In fact Jesus rarely did any of the roles that are commonly understood for spiritual leaders today. Nor does Jesus practice the modern how-to techniques and marketing methodologies that fill endless books on leadership.

Instead Jesus asked people to follow him around as he told stories about His Father and a Kingdom that will never end. Jesus was a shepherd.

Shepherding in history

To better understand what a shepherd is and does we have to return to the role of shepherd in biblical times – the time of Abel, Abraham,

Isaac, Jacob, Joseph, Moses, David and Amos. These were the original shepherds of the Bible, called from the fields to lead the flock of God.

Shepherding dates back thousands of years and we must see it as it was understood in history.

To fully appreciate God's call to spiritual shepherding we must grasp at least three essential historical characteristics of ancient Near Eastern shepherding:

1. a nomadic way of life
2. a family occupation
3. a need for one chief or head shepherd.

Nomadic people.

Ancient shepherds were a nomadic and semi-nomadic people. They were wanderers. Shepherding was a way of life. The sheep, flock and fold were their livelihood, their home. Put another way, there was no life apart from the flock.

This is vital to understand: the sheep and the family were wandering together as a kind of community; always moving, always growing, always responding to and for one another. The health and vitality of one affected all. The skill of the shepherd to lead the flock from pasture to pasture, clear water to cool streams was vital for their well-being. The shepherd had to know where he was going and how to protect the flock as they went. The life of the community depended upon it.

The nature of shepherding is change – constant movement, constant growth. A shepherd and flock are always growing, always moving toward fresh pasture and water.

So it is for the church today. The church cannot stand still. It is never a building. The church is an organism, actively living and spiritually growing. Either it grows toward Christ and a community of faith, or it wanders and falls away. To stand still is to starve. To divide will bring certain harm. It is the task of the shepherd-leader to lead the flock to living waters – to grow in Christ.

Family occupation.

Shepherding was a family occupation, a life of constant tending, guarding and feeding. Each family member participated in the work to one extent or another. Since every family member had a vested interest in the health and unity of the flock, strength was in staying together, helping each other, by each person performing their given task. For instance, the Old Testament tells us the task of drawing water for the flock was entrusted to girls (as seen with Rachel in Gen. 26:6-10).

The call to Christian ministry is necessarily a call of a marriage and family to ministry. Further, it is a call to community. The church is a family, a community of faith in which every member of the Body has a vested interest. The needs of one, submit to the greater need of all.

While all play a role in tending the flock, family members were more rightly called "under-shepherds." There were various levels of shepherds, according to the size of the flock and the experience of the shepherd. But each flock had one leader, usually the father, who had ultimate responsibility for the care and safety of the sheep. He was the chief shepherd or the head shepherd. The head shepherd was responsible for overseeing the flock, not necessarily doing all that was needed to be done – all had a part in this, including the sheep – but ensuring that what needed to be done for the flock's sake was accomplished well.

A need for one chief or head shepherd

There can be no church without leaders, no flock without shepherd leaders. Scripture teaches that Christ is head of the church. Christ is Head Shepherd. The New Testament calls elders and pastors to be His under-shepherds, or what we will call shepherd leaders. There is a functional and spiritual authority that God gives to church leaders – but always, and only, under His authority.

When we refer to shepherd leaders in the church we are referring to the leadership team – all the leaders in the church – not simply the pastor. There is no Chief Shepherd but Christ. All leaders are under-shepherds.

Shepherd-leadership takes place when a team of people employ various and complementary gifts to guide the church. Scripture distinguishes leadership as a spiritual gift. However, not all leadership positions require the leadership gift. Rather, Scripture emphasizes each part, and each gift, working together as a whole to build the Body up. In fact, as we will see later, Scripture places primary concern on the character of a leader, not gifting. Here, we begin to see how the role of a shepherd qualifies and expands our common notion of leadership from what the leader does to who the leader is.

In this section we will look briefly at the roles of a shepherd from history then explore how these descriptions carry over into our Old and New Testament understanding of spiritual leadership. In chapter one we will describe the tasks and responsibilities of a shepherd then look at

David as a model for shepherd leadership. We will note, briefly, how shepherding is similar to parenting in purpose and function. Chapter one ends with a discussion about recognizing who should lead, which will be discussed in more detail in chapter two.

Chapter One:
A Look at Shepherding

He chose David his servant and took him from the sheep pens;
from tending the sheep he brought him to be the shepherd of
his people Jacob, of Israel his inheritance. And David
shepherded them with integrity of heart; with skillful
hands he led them. Psalm 78: 70-72

In the introduction to this section we explored briefly how the historical role of a Near Eastern Shepherd begins to shape our under-standing of leadership. We now turn to how the specific tasks and responsibilities required of a shepherd illustrate our call to spiritual care.

Discernment & Decision Making.
Shepherd-leaders were responsible for making good decisions. This required wisdom and discernment – a kind of intuition that comes from hands-on experience. The shepherd had to choose which direction the flock would take each day.

The shepherd leaders led the flock by experience and instinct. Seasonal migrations brought the flock time and again over familiar lands. The shepherds knew from experience how to read the land and the weather ahead, where and how to find water for drink, pasture for feed, caves and sheepfold for protection, shelter in time of cold or storm, and shade from the burning heat of sun.

Each morning and evening the shepherds went to a high spot to view the land before them and to chart the next day's course. They had the wisdom and the responsibility to decide what the best course for the flock would be.

Scripture illustrates this point in the story of Lot and Abraham when it became clear that they needed to go separate ways. You can picture the two shepherds up on the mountain, surveying the great land spread out before them, choosing which way they would go.

Shepherd leaders survey the land and make decisions – based on what they see, interpret or know from experience. The book of Genesis illustrates this as Lot chooses a land and direction separate from Abraham. Lot chose what he saw to be good, but Abraham's vision came from God.

The spiritual shepherd leader leads by listening for God's voice and obeying His call. The experience and instinct of the spiritual shepherd leader is in hearing God's voice, not merely recognizing the "land" before him.

Leading.

The shepherds led. They led by going before, walking in front of the sheep. There is a great gulf between our Western idea of shepherding and the Syrian or Near Eastern way of tending sheep. The Western shepherd herds. He drives his sheep in and out like cows, usually on horseback with border collies running nervous circles around the sheep in the same way cowboys drive cattle.

But the Syrian shepherd led. He did not drive his sheep. The sheep willingly followed like loyal pets. In fact, the Near Eastern shepherd knew his sheep so well that he could lead them merely with his voice, a flute or whistle.

In a large flock the head shepherd went before the sheep and the family under-shepherds went with the sheep. The head shepherd never went behind. And the under-shepherds never pushed or drove the sheep. Just as the head shepherd could not go behind, he could not go too far ahead either. He led the sheep in a direction and at a pace sensitive to their need. The shepherd knew his flock. He knew when nursing ewes and weaker lambs required a change of pace and special attention.

Isaiah pictures the Good Shepherd who knows the needs of his sheep, carrying the weak, going slower for those with young.

The Psalmist notes how weaker sheep were often carried, "save your people and bless your inheritance; be their shepherd and carry them forever." (Ps. 28:9)

Care and safety.

Protection for the sheep was the shepherd's first concern. Every animal represented wealth and survival. Every lost sheep made the family poorer. A rod and sling were weapons against predators. The shepherd would risk his own life to defend his sheep as a father would his own son. So too, a pastor defends the flock as the family of God.

Calling & naming.

The Near Eastern shepherd knew his sheep by name. Every shepherd had a distinct call for his sheep. Each animal had a unique name and knew the shepherd's voice. The shepherd's voice brought calm and peace to the flock. When the shepherd approached the sheep his voice gave assurance that all was well. The sheep knew the shepherd's voice and would come instantly when called. Such trust the sheep had in the shepherd that no other shepherd calling that sheep's name could attract it.

Sheep fold.

The sheepfold was a simple roofless structure made out of rocks piled like New England border walls confining an area. The fold was enclosed on all sides with one opening in the front where the shepherd slept at night. Entering the fold by the gate, a shepherd counted the sheep each night. By lying in the sheep gate the shepherd could detect any movement from the sheep or threat from predators. The shepherd was watchman and gatekeeper to the sheep. Near Eastern shepherds often gathered their flocks together in a sheepfold at night, offering the shepherds fellowship and the sheep mutual protection.

Village Shepherd.

When we come to the time of Jesus, nomadic shepherding falls into decline. People were settling in villages and cities and the role of the shepherd changed. There became what were known as "village shepherds." The village shepherd was one person under whose care all the village sheep were placed.

Each morning the village shepherd would lead the sheep out and bring them back at nightfall. When under his care, the shepherd was responsible and liable for every animal. He was responsible to pay for any loss. Since he was a hired hand and not the owner of the sheep, loyalty both of sheep to shepherd and shepherd to sheep was sometimes lacking.

Jesus draws sharp distinction between nomadic and village shepherding. The shepherd leader cannot be a hired hand, but a loving parent, a sheep, like others, under the headship of Christ.

As we look to the Old and New Testament Scriptures, it is the Near Eastern shepherd model to which God speaks and which Israel, the apostles and early church understood. Keeping the tasks of the Near Eastern shepherd in mind as a model, let's look at a few of the many references in Scripture to shepherding and sheep.

Old Testament: God as Shepherd / Israel as sheep

In the Old Testament, Israel is continually reminded of Jehovah acting as Shepherd, the One Who leads in love: "In your unfailing love you will lead the people you have redeemed. In your strength you will guide them to your holy dwelling." (Ex. 15:13)

The familiar verses from Psalm 23 remind us, "the LORD is my shepherd, I shall not be in want." God is our comfort and restoration; our guide and our promise that "goodness and love will follow" us now and forever.

Just as Jehovah is pictured as Shepherd, Israel is continually portrayed as wayward sheep, apt to wander: "we all, like sheep, have gone astray, each of us has turned to his own way; and the LORD has laid on him the iniquity of us all." (Isa. 53:6; see also Jer. 14:10; Zech. 10:2)

These are but a few of the hundreds of verses throughout the Old Testament which use the language of shepherding to speak of God's present and future care for those He loves.

Other images of shepherding appear in reference to man. Kings and prophets are condemned for their inattention and greed as shepherds. Scripture reserves harsh words for those false shepherds of Israel who do not care for the sheep, promising a future justice when God raises up a Shepherd in the line of David.

Jeremiah and Isaiah proclaim a coming Messiah as well, One who will be both sacrificial Lamb and ruling Shepherd.

New Testament: the Lamb of God & Chief Shepherd

The Gospels point to Jesus as the fulfillment of prophecy, "Look the Lamb of God, who takes away the sin of the world." (John 1: 29)

Throughout the New Testament, Jesus Christ is portrayed as Shepherd and Lamb. He who tends the sheep for sacrifice is Himself the perfect sacrifice. He is the Provision, Abraham's "Jehovah Jireh" – the Lord will Provide. As Jonathan Edwards aptly says, God is both "purchaser and price."

One of the great mysteries of Scripture is the incarnation of our Savior. Jesus, the Living Word, very Son of God, takes on flesh, humbling Himself to become a man, even to the point of death. The Shepherd becomes the Lamb.

Inherent within the concept of leadership is being led. As Jesus came to do the Father's will, so too he called his disciples to "follow me," then sent them out into all the world calling others to follow the way of the cross. The Good Shepherd lays down His life for the sheep. What the ancient Near Eastern shepherds did for the safety of their flock, Jesus does for us.

In the New Testament, the Greek root word for shepherd means to feed, to rule and to nourish. A spiritual leader is called to guide and nurture the flock. Jesus Christ is the fulfillment and supreme role model of the Good Shepherd. (John 10) Just as His incarnation redeems and perfects manhood, Jesus transforms our view of leadership from power to love. Jesus is the One True Shepherd Leader.

David, a man after God's own heart

The description of David's call to ministry may offer insight into the preparation and requirements of a shepherd leader. "He chose David his servant and took him from the sheep pens; from tending the sheep he brought him to be the shepherd of his people Jacob, of Israel his inheritance. And David shepherded them with integrity of heart; with skillful hands he led them." (Psalm 78: 70-72)

Shepherding requires heart and skills, in that order. Unlike the role of prophet, priest or king, shepherding is about the heart first, not the head nor the hand. A shepherd uniquely combines images of power and gentleness, of authority and servanthood, of honor and humility. Shepherding starts with the heart, that is, with character. Scripture describes David's leadership by the words "integrity of heart." Integrity was the attribute of character that guided David's discernment, decision-making and practice of leading. Integrity links the shepherd to the sheep. Without integrity, the leader is a "hired hand," not a shepherd. Integrity is one of the essential attributes of every spiritual leader.

The Hebrew word for integrity is completeness, taken from a root word meaning to finish, complete or to be whole. Integrity is about actions and attitudes that are sound, upright or righteous. The English word for "integrity" comes from the word "integer" referring to a "whole number," a "complete entity," or something "undivided." In the church, integrity is being undivided in your relationship to God, yourself and others. It requires community, a collective commitment to "one Lord, one faith, one baptism; one God and Father of all, who is over all and through all and in all."

Spiritual integrity, or oneness, is a common theme throughout Scripture, with metaphors such as marriage and the Trinity illustrating the call to be one. Isaiah says that God will rejoice over Israel as a bridegroom rejoices over his bride (Isa. 62:11). Both Old and New Testament speak of apostasy (going after idols) as "adultery." The apostle Paul speaks of the mystery of "two becoming one" in marriage and the church.

In John 17, Jesus prays that the church might be one, linking our oneness with each other to the unity of the Godhead. The apostle Paul echoes Jesus' prayer when he urges the believer to be "like-minded," literally "of one mind," or "of one accord." Oneness is a frequent admonition and description in the writings of Paul, "have this mind in you which was also in Christ Jesus. . ." The model Christ sets is brokenness and humility.

Here, in Christ, we find the difference between shepherd and hired hand. The shepherd cares for the sheep before him/herself while the hired hand places personal interests above the interests of others. Whenever a leader's attitude or actions are self-protecting or self-serving, integrity is broken. The leader becomes a hired hand.

In addition to character, shepherding is a skill one cannot learn in the Temple, nor in a seminary. Shepherding is not, primarily, knowledge based. Rather, shepherding is a craft, a discipline, acquired over time living with the sheep under the tutelage of a head shepherd. When we look at what a shepherd is and does we begin to find how limited our understanding really is – and how far we have drifted from the biblical ideal.

The role of shepherd requires gifts and sensibilities that are often contradictory to our modern mindset, even impossible to render without God's enabling.

A shepherd leader, for example, must lead with authority yet humbly sacrifice. These traits are rarely found in one person. Today, the most "successful" churches have pastors with strong personalities, exceptional gifts and definite ideas. They, like King Saul, stand taller than the rest, exuding confidence and success. These are highly skilled visionaries, motivators and leaders. Often, however, they are aloof and relationally removed from most of their congregation.

A few decades ago the model was different. The ideal pastor then was a man of mercy who knew and loved everyone by name. Often, however, the man was not a leader and his fear of change and indecision bred confusion in the church. God's design for a shepherd leader combines skill and heart, strength and gentleness. The shepherd-leader is powerful yet humble, the greatest as well as the least.

A spiritual parent

Perhaps church leaders are called to shepherd because of all models, a shepherd is most like our Loving Father. Shepherding is much like being a parent, involving the same instincts, attributes and sensitivities of a godly mother and father.

The apostle Paul said as much in his epistles: " I am not writing this to shame you, but to warn you, as my dear children. Even though you have ten thousand guardians in Christ, you do not have many fathers, for in Christ Jesus I became your father through the gospel. Therefore I urge you to imitate me." (1Cor. 4:14-16)

Paul was both mother and father –a spiritual parent. But Paul does more than use the imagery. He makes a point to link leadership and effective parenting together, saying a spiritual leader must "manage his own family well and see that his children obey him with proper respect. (If anyone does not know how to manage his own family, how can he take care of God's church? – 1Tim. 3: 4-5)

Parenting, Paul states, is one of the qualifications or tests for leadership – both deacon and elder. Leaders demonstrate their character and leadership in the home first. Paul is saying that an ineffective parent should not serve as a leader.

Why does Paul place so much emphasis here? Is parenting a special litmus test for leaders? No, it is because leaders are "parents" to the flock, just as they are parents in the home. You are in the church what you are in the home.

When I was a student in graduate school I worked mornings as a garbage man. It was the perfect job for students – high pay, minimum hours and all you could eat. Garbage collecting taught me that you can learn about a person by what he throws away. You know what, when and how much he eats, drinks, reads, writes, buys and values. You know what he did last weekend and what he might do tonight. You can predict his income, his lifestyle, even how he might vote – all by what is in the garbage can.

If you really want to know someone, see them in their home – look at what goes in and what comes out. This is a modern way of saying what Paul was telling Timothy. Leadership starts at home. If you want to know a leader, look at his or her home. As the home goes, so goes the leadership.

How many spiritual leaders would have to leave ministry if they were obedient to God's Word? How much more would a pastoral search committee learn about a candidate by interviewing the pastor's spouse and children inside their home. Scripture is clear. If your home is in disarray, you cannot and should not lead in the church.

When Hezekiah's health was failing, God sent the prophet Isaiah to tell him to put his house in order. (2 Kings 20:1) Hezekiah, who was a righteous king, wept before the Lord and asked to live. The Lord added 15 years to Hezekiah's life. But Hezekiah did not put his house in order. He courted favor with Babylon and sinned against the Lord. During this time Hezekiah had a son named Manasseh. Crowned king at age 12, after his father died, Manasseh became one of the most evil, detestable kings in Israel's history, undoing all the good his father had done.

This lesson is a warning for leaders to be faithful to the end. God requires order. God calls you to obedience. It is not that good leaders cannot have difficulty in their families, or that sin is always the cause of problems, rather the lesson for us is that it is God's command and a sign of His direction that a leader with problems in the home must attend to those problems first, and if need be, resign or forfeit leadership in the church for a time. It is for the sake of the leader, as well as the church, that God gives this instruction: "put your house in order."

Here again, the shepherding model separates itself from modern notions of successful leadership, where marriage and parenting are private matters, irrelevant to performance. In the church, the private world reveals the true public figure.

Seen in this light, much could be said about the twin-track decline in church and home leadership over the past few decades. The church has in many ways become a mirror, instead of a corrective, to the dysfunctional family. Dysfunctional fathers and mothers raise dysfunctional churches as well as children. Most churches are very lax on these standards, turning a blind eye to what happens in the home. The church ignores clear signals of unhealthy and dysfunctional homes where, on the one hand, parents are so overly strict that they exasperate, even abuse their children and, on the other hand, parents who are so lenient that their children run wild.

Here again, the church is following our culture instead of shaping it. Parenting, we assume, is a private matter. We separate home life from church life. The New Testament makes no such separation. A child's character is formed in home and church.

When parenting is private, an open discussion about our marriages and children becomes off limits, engendering conflict over tolerance, rights and fairness. For instance, we served a church recently where the former pastor was "run out of town" because he separated from, then divorced his wife to marry another woman. Many in the church felt it was a private matter that should be forgiven. They saw no reason why the pastor should leave. Further, any who questioned the pastor were said to be judgmental.

There is no privacy in the church. We are called together to work out our salvation with fear and trembling. That means opening our lives to the good, the bad and the undiscussable. When the church becomes the church, leaders and members alike are committed to change and growth in submission to the Lord Jesus Christ. When a leader struggles it is a shared struggle. He or she can step down from ministry – not as a judgment or punishment, but as a means to have others come alongside. It is the logical result of biblical submission and one another love.

This is not what happens in our churches because we are not the church. We are Americans, private individuals with rights. This is why, as we will see more later, the church does not and cannot practice loving rebuke, correction and encouragement. Discipline requires a relationship and trust that does not exist; assumed but rarely practiced. It is not possible to implement godly discipline where this fellowship is lacking. When correction is required, the leader usually resigns or leaves the church before the discipline can ever be applied. Often he takes a contingent with him who are upset at how the church could be so hurtful.

Do you see how far we have moved from biblical community? Do you see the tremendous impact this has on even the simplest of matters? Correction and discipline are essential for life and learning. Both assume fellowship with God and one another. A leader cannot lead biblically outside of authentic Christian community.

We must love, come alongside and support people whose marriages are failing or whose children are rebelling. But Scripture is clear, these parents ought not and should not be leaders when this is occurring. If we are not practicing community before it happens there will be a fight and hard feelings when it does happen.

The church must stand in bold contrast to a world where divorce is rampant and families are falling apart. The church and its leadership must model stability and love through heartache and struggle. Again, the point is not that Christian leaders do not have marriage and family trouble. They do. "In this world you will have trouble," Jesus tells His disciples, "But take heart! I have overcome the world."

Shepherd leaders model Christ's overcoming grace. They model first in the home, in their relationship with their spouse, their children and their extended families, then in the Body.

With this background and description, we can learn how to recognize who should lead.

Chapter One Review:

In this chapter we looked at the historical and biblical model for shepherding, making application to the role of a spiritual leader in the church. As you reflect on what you have read, use the questions below to process what you have learned:

How has your thinking about leadership been challenged or changed by the role of a shepherd?

What single thought or image stood out to you as you read?

In your own words, write a statement or phrase that summarizes why God calls spiritual leaders to be shepherds:

This chapter explored how parenting relates to shepherding, and is a sign of leadership. Do you agree? When you consider your marriage, parenting or important relationships, what is God revealing to you about your leadership? Where are you weak? Where are you strong?

Chapter Two:
How to Recognize Who Should Lead

Then I will give you shepherds after my own heart, who will lead
you with knowledge and understanding. Jeremiah 3:15

Most common notions about leadership place authority in a person occupying a position. A leader has power by virtue of the title he or she bears, i.e., boss, pastor, parent and so on. This hierarchical approach tends to ignore the competency or character that is requisite for leadership, often placing people in leadership positions who are not skilled leaders.

In the church we muddle this even more by claiming that "everyone is a leader" in some capacity. As one Christian college President proudly proclaimed, "all of our students are leaders." Clearly, if words have meaning "all" cannot be leaders for the same reason one cannot say "everyone is above average." Leadership infers followers in the same way "average" requires some greater and some less.

Similarly, words like "authority" and "submission" have become so negative that they are largely ignored in Western culture. Each implies a controlling relationship, known more for law than grace, for coercion and abuse of power more than service. Church traditions and structures also color understanding. The Roman Catholic tradition, for instance, places special authority in pope or priest while some Pentecostal and fundamentalist church leaders claim unquestioned "anointing."

All of these factors present misunderstanding and confusion in following biblical commands for mutual submission and leadership authority. With shepherds and sheep there is no confusion. A shepherd leader model helps us understand the nature and function of spiritual leadership, lending specific ways for us to recognize, affirm and measure spiritual authority in our leaders.

Many questions arise: Who is a leader? What is authority? When, and in what ways, is it biblical to question a leader? How do we hold a leader in honor, yet accountable?

Before we can answer these and other questions we must understand the nature of authority, then turn to specific teaching in Scripture about spiritual authority. When we have surveyed these concepts we will move on to suggest ways to define and test spiritual authority in the church.

Five kinds of authority

There are at least five kinds of authority granted to man in Scripture: experiential, relational, positional, constitutional and spiritual authority. A brief definition of each will suffice:

Experiential authority is status or standing that recognizes previous experience, knowledge or expertise in a given field or specialty. A Pharisee by training, for instance, was an expert in the law and had authority to teach that others did not. The apostle Paul appeals to this, while citing its folly, in his letter to the Philippian church.

Relational authority is status by trust or relationship. In the Old Testament, kings and priests had familial origins. Only men from the tribe of Levi could be priests. The sons of kings inherited, or stole, their father's rule. The New Testament upholds relational authority in the home.

Positional authority is status or standing delegated by title, position or election. Scripture recognizes this authority in civil and secular leaders as well. The centurion who visits Jesus also speaks of this authority. (Matt 8: 5-10)

Constitutional authority is status or standing delegated by a constitution or by-laws. In denominations this is often referred to as constituted authority or, in military terms, "chain of command." In Acts 15, Paul and Barnabas appeal to the leadership in Jerusalem to hear their case.

Finally, spiritual authority is standing by grace received from the Holy Spirit. Some refer to this authority as an anointing, but this language creates more confusion than help.

Scripture teaches that all authority – whether experiential, relational, positional, constitutional, or spiritual – comes from God and requires our submission.

While each is from God and requires honor, the New Testament emphasizes church leadership based upon spiritual authority over experiential, positional, relational, and constitutional authority.

Spiritual authority is located in God's grace operating by faith in and through the believer. The authority of a follower or leader is not a possession or a position, but the empowering of the Holy Spirit manifest through the call, gifts and fruit of the believer's walk in the Spirit. Authority then, precedes leadership, and so, demands humility and responsibility. Humility, because the authority is God's, and responsibility because He entrusts it to man. There can be no room for selfishness. No room for personal gain. The prophet says "woe" to the leader who does not humbly lead. (Ezekiel 34)

Spiritual authority is a Spirit-gift of grace, a divine empowerment. It cannot be earned or learned. When we understand that spiritual authority is the Holy Spirit working in and manifest through a leader, we can begin to form ways of recognizing and testing where and when spiritual authority is present.

Surveying the biblical instructions and qualification for leadership we discover four components of spiritual leadership: calling, gifting, appointment, and character. We will demonstrate how spiritual authority is operative only when these four graces come together. We will see how a leader or follower may retain (and must be honored for) experiential, relational, positional and constitutional authority without these graces, but a leader cannot claim spiritual authority without the convergence of a spiritual call, gifting and appointment with godly character. That is, a leader cannot claim that he or she is speaking for God outside of the evidence and fruit of God's grace.

The rule of thumb is to recognize the place of authority. Experiential authority is in the experience. Relational authority is in the familial tradition. Positional authority is in the title and position. Constitutional authority is in the hierarchy established in by-laws. All these are established by God and conferred through the accomplishments or the status located in a person. We honor God by honoring the man or woman in authority.

However, spiritual authority is always located in the Spirit, never in the person. All honor, submission and obedience is to the Lord, never to the man. God is the object and subject of the authority. To test the authority we must recognize the signs of the Spirit. Scripture indicates at least four tests for spiritual authority in a leader: a call, a gift, an appointment and godly character. Let's consider each of these tests in some depth.

Can you find any instance in Scripture where a man or woman came into the role of godly leadership by seeking or obtaining the position on their own? Perhaps there is an instance, but I cannot find one.

Of course, there are many examples of God allowing ungodly leaders to come into power in order to demonstrate God's sovereignty. Pharaoh, Scripture says, was raised up for such a purpose. Using the definitions for authority discussed in chapter one, Pharaoh had positional authority. Many others in Scripture became powerful based upon experiential or relational authority, or by contrivance for personal gain. But no righteous leader came apart from God's calling.

Spiritual Calling

The first sign of a true spiritual leader is a calling. God calls. For many leaders, like Abraham, Moses, Gideon and David, the call came by great surprise and was often received with some reluctance. Each time, God initiated the call to leadership. Jesus, Himself, can only lead under His Father's call: "No one takes this honor upon Himself; he must be called by God, just as Aaron was. So Christ also did not take upon himself the glory of becoming a high priest. But God said to him, "You are my Son; today I have become your Father." And he says in Hebrews (5: 4-6),"You are a priest forever, in the order of Melchizedek."

Scripture is clear. You cannot will your way to leadership. You cannot earn it, learn it or muster it up. You cannot confer godly leadership upon yourself or others.

The New Testament stresses God's "call" to leadership. John the Baptist was filled with the Holy Spirit "even from birth" and that he was called to go before the Lord "in the spirit of Elijah." (Luke 1:15-17) Jesus reminds the disciples, "You did not choose me, but I chose you and appointed you to go and bear fruit —fruit that will last." (John 15:16).

The call comes from God and from God alone. It must come before anyone leads. Being "called" to shepherd is so like shepherding itself. To one who has heard God's call to lead, there is both comfort and humility. There can never be pride in leadership because the leader leads through no merit of his own, but by God's grace alone. To the one who has not been called to lead, there is grace to wait.

My wife, Sharon, likens a calling to the instructions we gave our children when they were young. Our farm rests on six acres of woods, pasture, hills and a brook. There was plenty of room for the children to run, hike and play. Nate and Sarah were free to enjoy everything within the boundaries of the property. But when Sharon called, they had to come.

As parents we want our children to explore, to discover and to learn all they can about everything within their interests and within certain defined boundaries. We do not want children idle, always sitting at our heels, waiting for a call. Such requirements would be oppressive, even abusive.

So it is with the believer seeking God. We are to move about within boundaries with the certainty that we are free under God's sovereignty. All that we truly need to know, God will place before us. What we do not know, we do not need to know.

God gives us boundaries in Scripture and in our heart. Often there is great latitude for us to explore and freedom that God expects us to pursue. The parable of the talents teaches this very point. Work the work God gives you. Explore all possibilities at your disposal. But always, be ever ready to come to Him when called.

Here is where good people often go astray, by taking their freedom to be a call. The possession of an education, gifts, experience or training does equal a call.

Yet it often happens like this: a person wants to serve God. He quits his job perhaps or graduates from high school and goes to a Bible institute or seminary. His motives are pure and his heart is sincere. He sacrifices much for God. He is humbled by receiving financial help from family and friends for study, to whom he says, "I'm preparing to be a pastor."

None of this is wrong . . . yet. Bible training is good for everyone and every calling. But in time, his assumptions about ministry and his assertion to others – words of his own making – come to be the same as the voice of God. "Why would God allow me to do all of this if He didn't want me to pastor?" he reasons. "Didn't I sacrifice? Didn't I give up good things for God?"

Finally, he graduates and accepts a church, or worse, starts one on his own. Soon frustration and difficulty come. People don't listen or follow. The power of his self-confidence and enthusiasm is lost. Then one morning he wakes up with a frightful realization. He has not been called. He is where he is by his own design and in his own strength. There is no more frightful place to be than outside of God's call. You will certainly fail.

What went wrong? Was it sinful to pursue the ministry or to study at college or seminary. No! Scripture tells us that those who aspire to leadership aspire to a good thing. But aspirations are not enough. The sin was in presuming these equal a call. An investment of time and energy, while laudable, does not equal readiness, nor a call. No degree can affirm or earn the qualification to lead.

Sheep, like playing children, are free everywhere inside the boundary set by the shepherd. They can graze and grow in peace and safety. But when the shepherd calls, the sheep must come. So it is with ministry. It is God Who calls. A person cannot call him/herself to ministry. All seeking to serve, however good, is chaff in the wind without a call. Why? Because leadership is first and foremost a calling from the Shepherd.

Ability does not equal a call.

If education does not equal a call, neither does ability. We cannot confuse capability with calling.

The ability to lead does not, in itself, equal a call. A call is not an ability to do something, however skilled you are at doing it. A call is God saying, "do this." I have learned by many trials and errors that there is a vast difference between God's call to action and my will for change.

Having the insight, experience or gift to see a problem, does not equal a call to solve the problem. An opinion is different than a call, and knowing what to do is separate from being told to do it. God is sovereign and He calls us first to love Him and second to love those He loves. We must conform our opinions and our solutions to God's will.

Stephen, in his speech before the Sanhedrin, illustrates this difference as he recounts God's work in the life of Moses (Acts 7: 20-36). Stephen tells us Moses was no ordinary child. He was wise and powerful in word and speech. In fact, Moses knew that he was gifted. "He thought that his own people would realize that God was using him to rescue them," Stephen says. But the Israelites did not recognize this because Moses was merely able, not called.

Not until forty years later did God call Moses. Was Moses equipped to serve forty years earlier? Probably. But that was not God's call nor purpose for his life. God had more for Moses to learn than stopping fights. Look where God sent Moses to prepare him to lead! To the wilderness tending sheep!

It is the call that must come first and foremost, not our abilities.

Are you called to be where you are? Or are you there merely by your skills and interests? The truthful leader must ask this question and answer honestly. No amount of personal investment, planning, time or ability is worth being outside of God's will. You have no right to do something God has not called you to do, however "able" you are to do it. It is obedience and loving submission that God is after in your life, not good intentions nor accomplishment. Go back within the boundaries of God's will and listen for his call.

Who says so?

Until now we have described what a call is and how to recognize it. But who determines who is called? To answer this, several points should be made.

First, every Christian has a general calling out of the world and into the church. To believe in Jesus is to surrender your life to His Lordship. To be Christian is to be a called out, called together person. It is in and through the church, the community of faith, that God calls believers to work.

Second, in the church each believer is called to ministry by works of grace. Upon conversion, every believer is gifted by God with spiritual grace (or gifts) to serve the Master. Spiritual gifts are given to accomplish our call. The call is what we do. Gifts are how we do it.

Third, a call is initiated by God. It is a gift. God calls us to service. Scripture gives no set pattern of formula for a call. A call can come through a sudden audible voice, such as with Paul on the road to Damascus. For others, the call comes through a series of events or prompting over time. Some hear God's voice directly, others through the words of another. For many, the fulfillment of the call comes years after it was first given.

What is common to all the calls in Scripture is that each person recognizes God as the source of the call. This is easy to understand and accept for Old and New Testament Scripture. We have no need to dispute what men and women heard in the first century. But who determines what God is saying today?

Fourth, God's call is affirmed in the church. It is the church gathered that recognizes and affirms a believer's calling. This was so from the time of Moses to the Apostles.

Fifth, a call is a way of life, not a vocation. While some hear God's call to vocational ministry, Scripture makes no distinction, as some do, between full and part time ministry. Paul affirms the role of the church to compensate Christian workers for their service, and to honor those who are in authority, but there is no hint of a "professional clergy" in Scripture.

Finally, a call is not about you, it is about God and His glory. You must not believe God needs you for any task. God does not need your permission, your works, your love, your gifts, your faith, your theology, your plans, your experience, your formulas, your network, nor your holiness. He does not need you. Nothing you can do or say can complete His sovereignty. All is grace.

George MacDonald once wrote, "You must not imagine that the result depends on you. The question is, are you having a hand in the work God is doing. God will do His work in His time in His way. Our responsibility is merely to be ready and available and to go where He sends and do what comes our way."

We must separate our will, our self and our reputation from the purpose God calls us to. We must learn to discern His voice over the tumult of our world, our families and our accomplishments.

Beware of becoming your own spiritual ventriloquist – a person who talks to himself and attributes his own thoughts and words to God. The final test for a call is not the leader himself. While a call is personal, it is always affirmed in the Body of Christ through the evidence of gifts and character.

Spiritual Gifting

Just as all believers have a call, all followers of Jesus Christ are given gifts of grace. The Greek word "charisma" literally means a "gift of grace." To be "charismatic" means to have a giftedness from God. Spiritual gifts are not about your personality, talents or attraction. This is true for every believer and all gifts. All gifting is from God. Leadership in the church therefore, whether vocational or volunteer, must always relate to giftedness. The leaders lead in and through their gift.

Spiritual authority is the faithful exercise of God's grace according to faith. The Apostle Paul states that leadership is a spiritual gift – a gift of grace – separate from and equal to that of teaching, encouraging and giving. It is not clear from Scripture whether the gift is always distinct or employed in the use of other gifts. Does a person gifted in administration, for instance, exercise leadership by governing diligently?

We should not make any more or less of what God's Word says. In one sense, all people who govern diligently are leaders. But biblical leadership seems to imply more that governance. The Greek word for "leadership" used by Paul is "proistemi" meaning "to be over, superintend, protect, guard and care for." Leadership, Scripture teaches, is a kind of double-gift combining power and nurture. Leadership is never power alone. The one "who is over" must also "care" for those being led. This impacts form and function. A leader must lead in love.

Paul says the gift of leadership is different in quality, purpose and expression. It is a separate gift from serving, teaching and other gifts. Further, the gift of leadership is to be exercised, like all the other gifts, according to its kind. Just as servants are to serve and encouragers to encourage, so leaders must "govern diligently." The Greek word "spoude" means to be diligent. There is an urgency and earnestness in this word, a pursuit to accomplish, promote and strive after something so that it may be done well.

Leaders are change agents. They are motivators. They are called by God to oversee what is done and ensure it is done well – with excellence – for God's glory. They are called by God's grace, by the power of the Holy Spirit. The person God calls to leadership will be equipped – gifted – by the Holy Spirit to lead. This is true throughout Scripture, in Old as well as New Testament. The empowering of the Spirit is found from Genesis to Revelation.

Two passages in the Old Testament illustrate how the Holy Spirit has in every age called and equipped leaders. God called Moses from the flock of Jethro to shepherd the nation of Israel, appearing to him in flames of fire within a bush. Moses was filled and empowered by God's Spirit to lead Israel out of Egypt and through the wilderness. He was God's shepherd-leader.

But, no sooner is the nation led out than the people start complaining. Moses grows weary, carrying the burden of the people alone. Finally, God says to Moses: "Bring me seventy of Israel's elders who are known to you as leaders and officials among the people. Have them come to the Tent of Meeting, that they may stand there with you. I will come down and speak with you there, and I will take of the Spirit that is on you and put the Spirit on them. They will help you carry the burden of the people so that you will not have to carry it alone." (Num 11: 16-17)

Notice how God equips the elders to serve by His Holy Spirit. The "elders" in this context literally means "older men," not a spiritual office. These were men who were honored and respected for their age and wisdom. They had relational authority, not positional authority. Moses confers upon them God's spiritual authority as under-shepherds to help carry the burden. The empowering comes from God. The same spiritual gift of leadership given to Moses was given to these elders.

Later, as the wilderness journey is coming to a close and Moses anticipates the crossing of the river Jordan and knowing he will not set foot in Canaan, Moses asks God to appoint a new leader. God sets apart Joshua, a man "in whom is the spirit."

The Old Testament leader led the nation, God's called out people, as keeper and reminder of God's covenant. When we come to the New Testament, God's enabling grace upon leaders is continued: "But you will receive power when the Holy Spirit comes on you; and you will be my witnesses in Jerusalem, and in all Judea and Samaria, and to the ends of the earth." (Acts 1:8)

Scripture teaches that the Holy Spirit endows leaders with various gifts, some with teaching, some with encouraging and some with other spiritual gifts. These are not innate "abilities" to lead, but divine enabling.

Gifts, neither abilities nor skills

In our psycho-therapeutic age, much is made of personality traits and behavioral dispositions. We all have traits that suggest the kind of person we will be and how we will relate to others. Social scientists have found ways to use these natural instincts to predict any number of outcomes, including what profession we will choose. The goal is to understand and so affirm ourselves to be confident in our profession. While these theories are interesting and even helpful as general guides, God does not factor personality nor self-confidence into gifting.

Gideon was overly cautious. Moses said, "Who me? The writer to the Hebrews tells us about many unlikely leaders throughout biblical history who are seen to "conquer kingdoms, administer justice. . . shut the mouths of lions, quench the fury of the flames, and escape the edge of the sword; whose weakness was turned to strength." (Hebrews 11:33,34)

The disciples were a rag-tag bunch of fishermen and penny-pinchers. Yet look at how God transformed them from followers into leaders in just forty days, from Golgotha to Pentecost. Each of the apostles led in various ways, according to their gifts, fleshed out through their person-ality. Peter was a leader. James was a teacher. John was an evangelist.

The apostles had positional authority established by Jesus, but they healed and spoke through spiritual authority given through the gifting and empowering presence of the Holy Spirit.

Gifts of grace, neither personal magnetism nor performance.

The Apostle Paul says "when I am weak, then I am strong" (2 Cur. 12:10f). Paul, who had the personality of a leader from birth and would have been a leader no matter what he did or believed, was given a "thorn in the flesh" as a reminder of his dependence upon God.

Christ Himself, it seems, had little or no human features that would attract people. "He had no beauty or majesty to attract us to him, nothing in his appearance that we should desire him." (Isaiah 52: 2f.) Neither Scripture, nor extra-biblical literature gives any hint that Jesus was in any way remarkable while growing up. It is striking that we know so little about Jesus' life before His public ministry. Jesus, it seems, was a classic "underachiever." This unknown man had little to credit his potential for leadership.

The resume' of the Messiah was in every way disappointing and unremarkable. Two thousand years later, the church would do well to review the lesson. Are we looking for and rewarding leaders by worldly or godly standards? "Not by might nor by power, but by my Spirit," says the LORD Almighty." (Zech. 4:6) When God calls men and women he gives them gifts to lead. Spiritual authority is a gift of grace.

Spiritual Appointment

Just as God calls out and gifts, He appoints the leader to a specific purpose and place to act. In Acts 13:2 the Holy Spirit instructs the disciples to "Set apart for me Barnabas and Saul for the work to which I have called them."

The Apostle Paul tells of his calling in Acts 26:10: "Now get up and stand on your feet. I have appeared to you to appoint you as a servant and as a witness of what you have seen of me and what I will show you."

To Timothy, Paul writes, "for this purpose I was appointed a herald and an apostle" (1Tim 2:7). In fact, in almost every epistle, Paul appeals to the authority of his divine appointment, not his own wisdom nor striving, as the basis for leadership, emphasizing he was "set apart" "by the will of God."

The same pattern emerges when we look closely at other spiritual leaders in Scripture. In each instance the call and gift are accompanied by an appointment.

As we look closer at these and other Scriptures we discover that spiritual appointment is often to a specific purpose and to a limited time or place. Joshua is appointed leader over Israel. Peter is to preach to the Jews while Paul is an apostle to the Gentiles. In other words, the call and gifting to lead does not extend an authority to lead in all circumstances and in every time and setting. The called and gifted must be appointed.

God has called a group of people to Metanoia Ministries to rebuild broken places in the evangelical church through leadership formation and conflict reconciliation. To do this, God gifts our workers with grace to discern and rebuke. We have a specific purpose for a particular kind of church that God has called us to serve.

But identifying who we serve does not grant us authority to serve. We have no authority to enter any church we like that meets our profile and tell them what's wrong or how to change. Nor do we feel we can give counsel to everyone who contacts our office. Spiritual wisdom and sound advice does not equal spiritual authority.

For these reasons and others, Metanoia Ministries has developed specific criteria to discern whether we have God's appointment to serve a given church. We don't want to be where we do not have God's appointment. If this sounds wise and humble, it is only because these are benefits that accrue from another motivation – fear. Scripture has harsh words for those who presume to speak for God outside of His appointment. (see Jer 6:14; 8:11; John 10:1; 2Tim 4:3)

A spiritual appointment to a specific purpose and place necessarily means we must constantly follow and depend upon the Spirit's leading. Paul makes this point from his missionary journeys: "Paul and his companions traveled throughout the region of Phrygia and Galatia, having been kept by the Holy Spirit from preaching the word in the province of Asia. When they came to the border of Mysia, they tried to enter Bithynia, but the Spirit of Jesus would not allow them to. So they passed by Mysia and went down to Troas." (Acts 16: 6-10)

Spiritual authority follows the Spirit's leading both to open and close doors of ministry.

Spiritual Character

If a spiritual call, gift and appointment opens the door to spiritual authority, the leader's character keeps the door open or closes it. Godly character accompanies and affirms spiritual authority. Here, unlike a call, gifting and appointment where God initiates and bestows, the leader participates in God's grace.

Character is the evidence and result of God's Spirit forming a man or woman. The believer is to take an active role by "walking " and "keeping in step" and "sowing to the Spirit" as Paul teaches in Galatians 5 and 6.

In Philippians, Paul exhorts the believer to "work out" his or her salvation "with fear and trembling" then goes on to describe the character traits to practice and avoid "so that you may become pure," like shining stars.

The context here, as in almost all of Scripture, is the community of faith. Character is formed in the church as the leader interacts, serves and submits to others under the Lordship of Jesus Christ. It is impossible to grow godly character outside the church, that is, the fellowship of believers.

The expectation of God in Scripture is that the leader will grow into Christ-likeness as he or she lives out and into his or her calling. (Eph 4: 1-4) It follows, and Scripture teaches, that the opposite is also true. A leader who fails morally or is persistent in willful or habitual sin forfeits spiritual authority. Character tests the authenticity of our walk with the Lord. (Gal 6: 7-8)

Here, again, is where the church must distinguish between spiritual authority and positional authority. A pastor or leader in the church has responsibility, but not spiritual authority, by virtue of his or her position alone. Positional authority must be honored and respected regardless of performance failures or character flaws. A bad leader is still a leader. Submission, as we will see, is unconditional.

However, no leader can claim spiritual authority when his or her life contradicts or does not evidence the fruit of God's Spirit. By spiritual authority here we mean "acting or speaking for God." God verifies His authority in part through the fruit of the leader's life.

The Apostle describes the kind of character expected of a spiritual leader in his letters to Timothy and Titus. "The reason I left you in Crete," Paul writes to Titus, "was that you might straighten out what was left unfinished and appoint elders in every town, as I directed you." (Titus 1:5) Titus' job was to appoint leaders. How was Titus to know who God wanted appointed? Paul says, "examine their character: you will know them by the fruit of their lives." Note that Paul mentions just one gift –

the gift of teaching – in the qualifications for elder. All the other qualifications are about character. If we combine the descriptions from Timothy and Titus we can create a list of character traits. (See 1Timothy 3: 2-12; Titus 1:5-9; Titus 2:7-8,15; Titus 3: 9-10.) The number or traits, like most lists in Scripture, is not the point, but rather the description. "This is what a godly, Spirit-filled leader looks like," says Paul, "a spiritual leader must be. . ."

- blameless: above reproach; holy; upright; loves good.
- marriage fidelity: the husband of one wife.
- good parent: managing home well; exemplified in obedient, respectful children.
- mature: not a new believer.
- good reputation: known and respected by unbelievers as well as believers; not a lover of money; not pursuing dishonest gain; honest in personal and business finance.
- gentle: peaceful; not overbearing, not quick-tempered or quarrelsome.
- hospitable: home open to needy.
- self-controlled: temperate; disciplined life; steadfast and stable.
- teach word: able to encourage by sound biblical wisdom and sound doctrine; able to explain God's word and to refute false teaching with boldness and wisdom.

Many churches use these character descriptions to select candidates for leadership, as they must. But the traits above are useful for discerning who should step down from leadership as well.

Apparently, Paul assumes that through the course of life people are going to have marriage, business and family concerns that take priority over the church. Rather than a punishment or disgrace these are guidelines for keeping first things first, for determining who God wants to serve the church and who needs to give more attention to their home.

This means that leadership should welcome and encourage a personal and corporate review of all leaders (including pastor) each year. When crises arise in homes, spiritual leaders must speak the truth to one another as well as come alongside in love and support. All leaders should have a "humble way out" of leadership using the character descriptions above.

Spiritual authority is recognized and affirmed by the church in a leader's call, gifting, appointment and godly character. When the apostles recognized the need for deacons they gave instruction to choose men whom the community recognized and affirmed as God's leaders: "Brothers, choose seven men from among you who are known to be full of the Spirit and wisdom." (Acts 6:3)

On Spiritual Authority

As we have demonstrated above, spiritual authority is resident in the operation of God's Spirit through a called, gifted and appointed man or woman who evidences godly character.

Spiritual authority does not rest in the position or even the person, but in the presence of the Holy Spirit. Authority frequently becomes a major point of misunderstanding, contention and deception in the church, impacting how we recruit, affirm and follow leaders – from pastors to elders to workers.

In contrast to the church affirming and forming leaders by their call, gift appointment and character, most churches employ a professional or secular, business model of organization. In this model, power is located in titles and positions – whether it is Chairman of the Board or Senior Pastor. In most churches the pastor is the Chief Executive Officer. This is true of traditional churches that have plateaued or are dying as well as the highly successful contemporary churches sprouting up across the country. This is problematic for reasons both functional and spiritual.

Functionally, few traditional pastors understand or are gifted in leadership. In the business world most would not rise above middle management and would never be recognized as a senior leader. In fact, the personality and motivation for people entering seminary training and the ministry is quite different from those who pursue business careers. When a church requires a traditional pastor to be CEO, the pastor and the church usually fail because it requires a pastor to perform in areas of weakness, not strength.

Many churches are beginning to recognize this and have taken steps to change. However, instead of questioning or changing the model, they change the leader.

The answer for the evangelical church in America now seems to be to recruit, train and hire Chief Executive Officer type pastors – only gifted communicators and charismatic leaders are welcome. Apparently, this "works." Churches with CEO type leaders seem to grow, at least in the short run. Having solved the functional problem we are now faced with a spiritual one. We have to ask, "what causes the growth?" Is it the model? the leader? or the leading of God's Spirit? All say it is God's blessing or work, but is it? How would we recognize the difference?

How does a professional orientation, founded upon secular principles, keep from being a professional, secular organization? How and where does the church draw the line between creating itself in man's image or God's? How does a market-driven model keep faithfulness, not performance, as it's standard to discern and test God's will?

A business, for instance, must keep changing to keep up. What works today likely will not work tomorrow. It must change to meet the market, and fill the need. This point is made by some to prove the irrelevancy of the church. Since businesses succeed by changing every three years to meet market needs, the argument goes, so should the church. Why? The church is founded upon a 4,000 year-old salvation story, the apex of which hangs on a 2,000 year old cross. The most innovative and effective businesses in the world are no more than 15, 25 or 100 years old. Worse, their longevity is owed more to the ability to conform and react, not transform.

Few evangelicals would advocate that the church become a business, at least in this sense. All affirm that the church is the Body of Christ, a living, organic, spiritual reality. But if we believe this, why not have a model for leadership and authority that is marked by biblical/spiritual standards, instead of secular principles?

Since most of our churches lack a biblical model, we are left to discern and decide as best we can, usually with subjective and arbitrary guidelines. The church errs by spiritualizing leadership as well as secularizing it.

Don't touch the "merchandise"

Some leaders, for reasons that are sincere, misguided or manipulative, often confuse positional authority with spiritual authority in order to demand obedience or compliance of members.

We have served numerous churches where leaders and members quoted verses such as "don't touch God's anointed," as reasons why they did not correct, rebuke or hold sinful leaders accountable. It is not uncommon for pastors to foster this false teaching for their own self-protection.

Scripture does warn against those who would challenge God's anointed servants. The "anointed" in 1 Samuel 24:6 refers to David's unwillingness to lift his hand against Saul, King of Israel. Here David speaks about not lifting his hand against the Lord's anointed king. However, David readily and frequently pleads his case against Saul, before God and before Saul himself. David is commended for giving honor and respect to the nation's first king.

In 1 Chronicles and Psalms, the specific command "do not touch my anointed ones" has nothing to do with leadership nor leadership anointing. Rather the "anointed ones" are all Israelites, all who believe and follow God. These texts are not about internal strife but warnings to unbelievers – people who are outside of the faith – about the consequences of challenging the people of God.

We must not muddle God's anointing with personal sin and failure. God's anointing in Scripture is about God, not people. The anointing oil symbolizes God's authority, not any power or authority resident in the person. It is grace and grace can never be an excuse for sin.

Unfortunately defensive and aggressive leaders will often use their position or title as a claim for special anointing or spiritual authority. This is especially true in churches that emphasize the mystery and manifestation of God's Spirit. We must be careful not to deny God's power falling upon and working through men and women, but we must always warn against conferring God's power to a person. God is always the object and subject of spiritual authority. Any claim otherwise is spiritual arrogance.

To claim special authority is to sin against God and His church. Against God because the authority is His. Against the church because the claim diverts attention from behavior to status.

Spiritual authority resides in God, not people and is affirmed and tested by spiritual fruit such as joy, peace, patience, gentleness, self-control and so on. There can be no room for selfishness, no room for personal gain. Indeed, any "spiritual" acts that are self-motivated are an abuse of authority.

Chapter Two Review:

In this chapter we looked at the call, gifting, appointment and character of a spiritual leader. As you reflect on what you have read, use the questions below to process what you have learned:

How did God call you to faith in Jesus Christ. Record below a brief timeline of your spiritual journey.

As you look at this timeline, how has God called or prepared you for ministry?

What spiritual gifts have others seen and affirmed in you?

Where has /is God appointing you to serve? In what ministry? In what place?

Look back on the character attributes mentioned above. Which of these attributes are you known for? Which of these attributes are you weak in?

After reading this chapter, what questions or observations do you have about spiritual authority?

SECTION TWO:
What Every Leader Must Always Do

He will stand and shepherd his flock in the strength of
the LORD, in the majesty of the name of the LORD his God.
And they will live securely, for then his greatness will reach
to the ends of the earth. Micah 5:4

In the previous section we discovered how to recognize and affirm spiritual leadership through a call, gifting, appointment and character. Having described who a leader is, or what he or she must be, our task now is to outline and describe what every leader must do. Here again we rely upon the model of a shepherd to guide our thinking. The primary task of a shepherd is to care for and nurture a flock. To accomplish this every shepherd had to oversee and to accomplish several key tasks, such as setting a course of direction, providing fresh food and water and so on. From these basic functions we can find related actions described in Scripture for leaders who would shepherd the church.

In this section, we will consider the role and task of a Shepherd Leader in seven areas:

1. Re-presenting Jesus Christ: making the Lordship of Jesus Christ the object and subject of all we do. Spiritual leaders do not represent the opinions, agendas, or needs of the congregation; they re-present the Lordship of Jesus Christ to the needs, issues, and decisions facing the church.

2. Embodying God's Vision: the process of hearing, discerning (from God's Word, His Spirit and His people), and living into God's vision for His Church (universal) and the local church in particular. We believe audition precedes vision, that is, leaders are responsible to hear, obey, and model what God is leading the church to be and do.

3. Defining Current Reality: discerning and speaking the truth in love; describing reality – where the church is in light of God's purpose and vision; acknowledging and confessing weaknesses as well as celebrating strengths; exposing sin and leading in correction, rebuke, and encouragement.

4. Setting and Keeping Boundaries: framing the boundaries within which the church will operate and grow. Boundaries provide safety, trust, and guidelines for measurement, correction, and encouragement.

5. Feeding and Nurturing the Flock: keeping watch and overseeing the nurture and health of the flock. Leaders must provide for physical, mental, emotional, and spiritual support and sustenance. This includes nourishment from hearing and describing God's Word, living and walking by His Spirit, and fellowship with His people.

6. Mentoring and Equipping Leaders: identifying, equipping, and mentoring gifted people to minister together interdependently. Empowering and equipping others to discover, use, and grow in their gifts to glorify God and to edify the Body.

7. Modeling and Forming Character: living out the character traits of Scripture, while calling others to transformation. For leadership, the virtues of brokenness, courage, integrity and justice are vital.

But before we review each of these functions, I want to reveal some of the assumptions and beliefs underlying these steps. I do so because I am fearful that the very act of naming or numbering "steps" will infer my support of a way of thinking that I am actually standing against. Let me explain.

For 18 years, I owned and operated a direct marketing and communications firm that served many organizations. Over those years we were involved in developing and implementing corporate identities with clearly defined mission, vision and strategic plans to advance the cause of the given organization. Our livelihood was linked to our ability to create innovative strategies that would reach and effectively persuade carefully targeted audiences. For the most part we were successful in harnessing and perfecting techniques to accomplish this. We were, as some might say, effective. Years ago, pastors and church leaders began asking us to bring this learning into the church. "How can our church be more effective?" we were asked. The question troubled me some, but not as much as it should have. We helped some churches to cast a vision and write a plan.

At the same time I began reading Stanley Hauerwas and others who opened up to me a way of thinking about the church as a "community of forgiven saints" whose witness stands in contrast to the world. I began asking, "what does it mean to be Christian?" and "what is God's purpose for the church?" When I explored principles of leadership in Scripture, looking for methods that I might teach to others, I became increasingly uncomfortable with my assumptions, particularly when confronted by the life and words of Jesus. The only surefire method I could find in Jesus was that there were no surefire methods, tools or techniques. More alarming was the discovery that effectiveness is a value of most North American, white, male, baby-boomers, but is not a value of Scripture. If we measured Jesus' earthly life by what we call "effectiveness," He must be one of the most ineffective leaders in history. For one thing, Jesus did not recognize good strategic advice when He got it from his brothers and disciples. (See Matthew 16: 22-23; John 7: 1-6).

I give this background to introduce why I have become increasingly alarmed at how the evangelical church has uncritically adopted method-ologies that, while effective in reaching people, may also be forming believers to think and to act like consumers, not followers of Jesus Christ.

Clearly this is unintended. Few pastors or church consultants are crass marketers. Rather, most are motivated by a passion to reach souls for Christ. Sincere statements such as, "To reach youth or single moms for Jesus, we have to find out who they are and what they need" reveal a zeal for evangelism too often lacking in the church. However, in our passion to communicate the Gospel are we minimizing the cost?

With zealous methods may come unintended, even counterproduc-tive results, as it did with Peter rebuking Jesus for talking about cruci-fixion. In the same way, we must guard against notions of leadership that would place human performance above spiritual ideals. When we do so, Jesus would say to us, "You do not have in mind the things of God, but the things of men." (Matthew 16:23)

In the following chapters, we will consider what every leader must always do. In each chapter we will explore why each task is essential and what happens in the church – for health or harm – as a result.

Chapter Three:
Re-presenting Jesus Christ

I will place over them one shepherd, my servant David,
and he will tend them; he will tend them and be their shepherd.
Ezekiel 34:23

Spiritual leaders do not represent the opinions, agendas, nor needs of the congregation; they re-present the Lordship of Jesus Christ to the needs, issues, and decisions facing the church. That is, they apply the Lordship of Jesus to every task, every decision and every situation. Spiritual leaders must make the Lordship of Jesus Christ the object and subject of all things.

Leaders invite others into an encounter with Jesus' Lordship. In the Greek Old Testament, the word, "Lord," appears more than 6,000 times in reference to the Hebrew name for God. Lordship means absolute trust and dependence upon Yahweh. To make Christ Lord is to give him full jurisdiction over all matters.

David Hansen, in his book, The Art of Pastoring, speaks about re-presenting Christ by describing the difference between a leader becoming parable versus a symbol. Most leaders want to be symbols. God calls us to be parables. Let's examine the difference: a symbol is permanent, a parable is temporary.

The cross of Jesus Christ is a symbol. When we look at the cross we are reminded of Jesus Christ crucified. We remember the cost of salvation — His grace, not our works. Jesus' life, death, and resurrection are the focus. The cross reminds us of our hope in Christ.

A parable is temporary. It serves as a picture that quickly goes away. So Jesus tells his disciples, " the kingdom is like a mustard seed. . . it starts out very small, but grows very large . . ." The mustard seed gives a picture. Once the picture is understood, the seed is unimportant. The subject is the Kingdom, not the seed. A parable is a picture that points to a subject, then gets out of the way.

Leaders are called to be parables, never symbols. To determine the difference, one can ask a simple question: "who is the object and who is the subject?" If the answer is the leader, an issue, a vote or anything but Christ, we have allowed parables to become symbols.

That is the art of spiritual leadership: to make Jesus Christ the object and the subject of everything we do. Never allow a decision, a success, a failure nor conflict to be about a leader. Always make the issue about submission to the Lordship of Jesus Christ. Point to Jesus and get out of the way.

Leading by Invitation

In Matthew 22, Jesus tells a story comparing the kingdom of heaven to a king who prepares a wedding banquet for his son. At the appointed time the king sent his servants to tell the invited guests that the dinner was prepared and that the banquet was ready. But the guests refused to come and abused the king's servants. This enraged the king. He sent his army to punish those guests whose response proved they did not deserve to come. Then the king sent his servants into the streets to invite all they could find to the banquet – both good and bad people – so the wedding hall was filled with guests.

Jesus spoke this parable against the Pharisees to illustrate how "many are invited, but few are chosen." Jesus' parable models a leadership style found throughout Scripture and essential for shepherding: leadership by invitation.

In Genesis four, God refuses the offering Cain brings to the Lord. To modern ears, this appears unfair. Cain was depressed. But God said to Cain, "Why are you angry? Why is your face downcast? If you do what is right, will you not be accepted? But if you do not do what is right, sin is crouching at your door; it desires to have you, but you must master it." (Gen 4:6-7) God invites Cain to do what is right. The invitation offers a pathway and proof of character. If Cain obeys he will be accepted and will prove his mastery over sin. But if Cain refuses, the true nature of his heart and his offering will be revealed.

Character, like faith, is always proved in submission.

Throughout Scripture we read similar stories where God poses questions that invite a response in order to reveal faith and to prove character.

Invitation is the best way to re-present Jesus Christ to discover truth, to correct sin or failure and to lead change.

The secret to leadership by invitation is this: always frame issues in the form of a question that invites submission into a spiritual discovery process for a specific, limited time.

Leaders must continually invite people into the discovery of a way of life that is shaped by the cross. For instance, restoring a sinner to fellowship should involve more than repentance. Invite the sinner to demonstrate his or her "good confession" by taking tangible steps to right the wrong and to transform his or her character. If the sinner refuses to do this, the true nature of his confession is revealed.

Invitation is essential for leading change. To apply this, let's consider the common problem of changing worship style in a church.

First, the leader must frame the real issue. For example, to change from a traditional to contemporary worship style, the leader must frame the issue around God, not form.

Second, the leader must present a question that invites submission. The leader does not pronounce or decree a change in worship style. Nor does a leader attempt to manipulate or coerce change through political means, quoting experts or declaring "this is God's will." Rather the leader invites the congregation to enter into the change process through submission. Refusing to submit is a different and larger problem than accepting change. Most resistance to change is really about submission, not change. A wise leader will recognize and address these separately.

Third, the leader invites submission to Jesus Christ. That is, the leader invites submission to a process of discovering God's will, not human will or opinion. The Lordship of Jesus Christ must always be the object and subject of the submission. "We believe God is prompting us to discover new ways to worship Him . . . would you join us as we discover how God might be leading us through His Word, His Spirit and His people?"

Fourth, the leader invites the congregation into a discovery process for a specific period of time. It is coercion, not leadership, to say, "from now on we'll be using guitars and drums instead of the organ." Leadership says, "for the next eight to ten weeks we will be introducing some new songs and instruments into our worship service. We invite you to join us in asking God to be Lord over our worship." (Most people will enter into change if the timeframe is not more that ten weeks. Less than seven weeks is not enough time to explore a change well. After ten weeks invite them to another ten!)

The kingdom of God is an invitation to worship that culminates in a great wedding supper of the Lamb. We ought to lead in such a way that invites others to the banquet.

Invitation & Location

Leadership is the art of inviting people into a way of life shaped by the cross. Great leaders always lead by describing, then inviting people into a life of obedience. Throughout the Gospels we find Jesus inviting Pharisees and disciples, Jews and Gentiles into a new way of hearing, seeing and acting. He describes a kingdom and invites people to follow.

Through Jesus we learn that invitation presupposes (and requires) location. To invite someone to follow presumes that journey can be located in a specific space, a certain story. The story, of course, is the Gospel – the salvation narrative that anticipates, announces and reveals Jesus as God's Son, the Messiah. Followers of Jesus are people who live by and participate in His story. We call ourselves Christian, but it is important to note that our story cannot be contained in a title. In fact, the word "Christian" only appears three times in Scripture. More importantly, the phrase "in Christ" is used hundreds of times to describe the spiritual posture and position of the believer. To be a follower of Jesus is to have one's heart, mind, and spiritual identity located in the reality and activity of Christ. Re-presenting Christ, therefore, means owning, telling and participating in the story of Jesus.

I once received a call from a pastor who had been fired from his church. The pastor had been badly mistreated by his congregation, and his hurt was great. He described several attempts at reconciliation; each was refused. Three years had passed and the pastor had still not felt release from his pain. He asked for my thoughts. I empathized with his feelings. We work with many pastors who are treated unfairly and hurt. "I understand you feel hurt," I said, "but I wonder why you are allowing the sin of others to squelch your faith?

"Well, I am hurt!" he responded.

"Yes. But what are you doing with your hurt?" I asked. "Is the hurt constructive or destructive?"

The pastor responded with more appeals for sympathy. He told me how others had failed him and wondered out loud how he could ever trust other believers again.

"You are telling the story of a victim," I said.

"I am a victim!" He quickly responded.

"Then you are not living the Christian story," I replied. "There are no victims – only overcomers – in the Christian story."

We went on to explore what it would look like for Christ to bear the pastor's pain, how to examine where his patterns of thinking and responses contributed to the problem, how forgiveness could release his past.

We talked about how, by holding onto his hurt, the pastor was actually living a story opposed to Christ, nullifying the power of the Gospel. "Jesus did not die so that you could feel sorry for yourself," I said. "You will not be healed until you stop thinking and acting like a pagan, and start thinking and acting like a Christian."

The Christian story locates our identity, reality, and activity in the life, death and resurrection of Jesus Christ, not in our circumstances. The story is not about us, but about Him. The call of a shepherd leader is to remember and tell the story Jesus.

Re-presenting Christ in prayer.

John Wesley once wrote, "Give me one-hundred preachers who fear nothing but sin and desire nothing but God, and I care not a straw whether they be clergymen or laymen; such alone will shake the gates of hell and set up the kingdom of heaven on earth. God does nothing but in answer to prayer."

Prayer is the primary work of every shepherd leader. Prayer is the practice of submitting our personal and corporate lives, issues, problems, joys and pains to the Lordship of Jesus Christ and to His work in and through the Church. To pray is to proclaim the Gospel.

The word intercede literally means "to go between parties and to reconcile differences." Intercession is a meeting. In prayer, a leader meets with God to apply the power of Jesus' resurrection to life concerns. Intercession re-presents Jesus to our situation.

James writes: "Is anyone among you suffering? Then he must pray. Is anyone cheerful? He is to sing praises. Is anyone among you sick? Then he must call for the elders of the church and they are to pray over him, anointing him with oil in the name of the Lord; and the prayer offered in faith will restore the one who is sick, and the Lord will raise him up, and if he has committed sins, they will be forgiven him. Therefore, confess your sins to one another, and pray for one another so that you may be healed. The effective prayer of a righteous man can accomplish much. Elijah was a man with a nature like ours, and he prayed earnestly that it would not rain, and it did not rain on the earth for three years and six months. Then he prayed again, and the sky poured rain and the earth produced its fruit." (James 5: 13-18)

When Moses, Joshua, Samuel and David faced a question, challenge, or critical decision they went to "inquire of the Lord." Literally, they "consulted" with God in prayer, "should we go up . . should we go down?" The promise and expectation was that God would answer when His people called.

The first followers of Jesus were known for their devotion to prayer. In the days leading up to and following Pentecost, believers were intent on prayer. "These all with one mind were continually devoting themselves to prayer, along with the women, and Mary the mother of Jesus, and with His brothers. . . They were continually devoting themselves to the apostles' teaching and to fellowship, to the breaking of bread and to prayer." (Acts 1:14; 2:42)

It is impossible to hear God's voice; discern His will, and make wise decisions without prayer.

Re-presenting Christ in Word.

The Psalmist writes: "You have exalted above all things, your Name and your Word." In prayer we call upon, praise and bless the Name of the Lord   In Scripture, we locate ourselves in Christ, the Word incarnate.

These twin duties – prayer and Word – were the focus of the first apostles. When confronted with the real need of Greek widows, the apostles urged the disciples to appoint people filled with the Spirit to serve, so that the apostles could continue to "devote ourselves to prayer and to the ministry of the Word." (Acts 6:4)

To be Christian, one must locate oneself in Christ, under His Word. The Shepherd Leader is one who places him/herself under, in order to draw discernment and direction from Scripture. When difficult times come, Paul says to Timothy, "continue in the things you have learned . . . and known from the sacred writings." Watch out, says Paul for men who follow a form of godliness – always learning but never knowing the full truth. Instead, Paul exhorts Timothy to look to Scripture for teaching, correction and training. The leader's adequacy and competence, then, is not in human performance and skill, nor in knowledge about the truth. Right character, or what Scripture calls "righteousness" comes by submission to the training of God's truth. This means engagement more than study or memory. It means entering into the story, allowing the story to claim you, direct you, even judge you. God's Word is living and active; it is the "sword of the Spirit" (Eph 6:17) able to judge thoughts and intentions. (Heb 4:12)

To represent Christ is to invite God's people into a life of discernment and obedience as, together, we place ourselves under the saving and sanctifying work of God through His Word, His Spirit and His people.

In prayer and Word we inquire of God in order to display the Lordship of Jesus Christ in our midst.

Chapter Three Review:

In this chapter we looked at the first of seven tasks every leader must always do. Meet with your leadership team to complete and discuss the following exercise. Read each statement. Using the scale provided, indicate how true each statement is for your leadership team. Indicate how you really feel (not what you think you ought to.) Ask yourself: "Does this statement describe our actual habits and practices?"

If the statement is always true, place the number 5 on the line in front of the statement. If the statement is never true, then write the number 0 on the line. Place the number (0-5) that is the most accurate description of your actual leadership practice.

SCALE
5 = Always true.
4 = Often true.
3 = Sometimes true.
2 = Seldom true.
1 = Almost never true.
0 = Never true.

Please answer these statements referring to your actual practice. Be honest. Don't hesitate to choose a 5 or 0. Avoid using 3.

Re-presenting Jesus Christ:
1) _____ The Lordship of Jesus is the object and subject of all we do.
2) _____ Jesus' Name and His Word is exalted above all things.
3) _____ We regularly submit our lives, decisions and leadership to God in prayer.
4) _____ We seek the Holy Spirit for discernment on all issues and decisions.
5) _____ We are open to new ideas and will take faith-filled risks.

Compare and discuss your responses, asking questions such as:

"Why? What is it about us that we are thinking or acting this way?"

"What is God saying to us that we need to hear?"

"How long has this been true about us?" or "When did this start?"

"What would we need to do to address these results?"

Chapter Four:
Embodying God's Vision. Or, Why
Overseers Must Be Under-hearers.

Therefore, you shepherds, hear the word of the LORD. Ezekiel 34:7

Valley Church had just nominated six new men to join their elder board. To introduce the new elders, one man was presented to the Body each week for six consecutive Sundays. Each man was asked to speak about two subjects: his spiritual journey, and his vision for the church.

As each man gave testimony to God's provision and grace in his life, the congregation renewed its collective commitment to the Salvation Story. People were drawn together. (We recommend having testimonies as a regular part of worship. There is great unity in the cross when we admit our faults and brokenness to one another.)

But the unity gained was soon lost when each man spoke about his vision for the church. After six weeks, there were six different visions.

Now, picture yourself in the open fields with a flock of sheep. There are six of you shepherding together, tending one flock. The pasture is well worn and it is time to move on. At this point one of your fellow-shepherds says, "follow me," and starts walking south. At the same time another shepherd says, "this way" and walks due north. Another goes northwest, and so on until each shepherd sets out in a different direction according to his "personal" vision for the flock. Everything a shepherd spends his life trying to avoid now occurs in the flock: confusion, distrust and separation.

Some sheep will follow one shepherd. Other sheep will follow another. Some sheep will start one way then turn to go another way. Ewes will realize their lambs are not with them and they will run back to where they started, searching frantically while getting lost.

The further each shepherd leads his sheep away, the worse the problem becomes. The shepherd will only be able to care for the sheep that follow him. Many will be lost, left to lead themselves.

With sheep on a hillside it is easy to see the folly. Yet we repeatedly make this same mistake in the church, with dire consequences. We ought to know better. The problem is ancient.

Moses was on the mountain receiving the ten commandments while Israel grew restless. Finally, the people stiff-armed Aaron to act saying, "make us gods who will go before us. As for this fellow Moses" they said, "who knows what has happened to him?"

So, Aaron created a golden calf as an idol for the people to worship. When Moses came down the mountain, the Scriptures say he "saw that the people were running wild and that Aaron had let them get out of control and so become a laughingstock of their enemies." (Exodus 32:15)

It is important to consider the threefold observation (and accusation) Moses made:

1) The people were running wild;
2) Aaron let them get out of control;
3) They became a laughingstock to their enemies.

This describes many of the conflicted churches we serve. Members are out of control because leaders have failed to lead. And unbelievers look on and laugh.

Revelation.

Churches, like nature, abhor a vacuum. Without a common purpose, direction and vision, a congregation, like sheep, will wander. A church without a clear, identifiable direction is a church without leadership. Worse, it is a church inviting confusion and division. Scripture puts it this way, "where there is no vision, the people perish." (Pr 29:18 KJV) In other words, without a vision, you're dead.

The NIV translates this verse closer to the original Hebrew, "Where there is no revelation, the people cast off restraint." The Hebrew word "para" literally means "to show lack of restraint, or to let loose restraints." A flock without clear direction will wander, each to its own way, resulting in chaos and confusion. Literally, the proverb warns, "Where there is no vision, the people are undisciplined or get out of hand."

Much of the disarray, bickering and fighting for control in our churches can be traced back to the absence of a compelling, shared vision – that is, a vision that a leadership team identifies, communicates and lives into.

When Metanoia Ministries is invited to assess a conflicted church, some of the first questions we ask leaders and members are these:

"Where is this church headed? What is your vision? Do you have one? Where will you be in five years?" In every conflicted church we have served, the answer was the same. "We don't have a vision."

Interestingly, most of the churches have gone through the process of writing a vision statement – often with great celebration – yet still find themselves in conflict. Why is this? Because a vision is not a statement; it is a way of life. The vision must be embodied. By embody we mean practiced. Having a vision is not the same as embodying the vision. "Knowing" your vision is a vital first step. But it is only the first step. Leadership must be the vision. That is, they must live into it, to model and exemplify what life would be like when guided by the vision. If your church does not have a clear and compelling vision that leadership is putting into practice, you will have conflict and confusion. Always.

Churches that embody a clear vision still have conflict. The difference between health and dysfunction is not the absence of conflict but the foundation on which the conflict is addressed. Leaders who embody vision, address the conflict consistent with the values and vision they are living. Trust hinges on the consistency of words to action.

There will always be honest differences between sincere Christians about how a church gets to where it is going. If there is no clearly articulated and practiced vision which all are called to assimilate, then the "how" becomes an argument for obtaining self-centered needs and personal preferences. Conflict, confusion and resentment result.

In Proverbs 29:18, the final phrase that offers the writer's remedy is often forgotten: "Where there is no revelation, the people cast off restraint; but blessed is he who keeps the law." Vision-casting requires law-keeping.

God has revealed a plan for what the church, His flock, is called to do and be. This vision is found in God's Word. A shepherd leader is called to study and to pray; to listen and to discern God's direction through His people and through His Word. Keeping watch means "keeping the law."

Listening to God: why audition precedes vision.

Many helpful books and articles have been written calling the church to a clear and compelling vision. The problem with much of the advice, however, is that it limits God's revelation to human effort – to marketing methodologies relying upon goals, tactics and "keys to success." This is not a biblical perspective. There are no methods in the Church of Jesus Christ.

The word audition, not vision, better describes the leader's role in understanding God's direction. The emphasis of Scripture is more often to hear and obey, rather than see and do. Webster defines "audition" as the power to hear or the sense of hearing; the act of hearing. Both the Hebrew word "shama" and the Greek word "akouo" meaning "to hear," carry with them a sense of action. The hearer not only hears, but discerns, interprets and obeys. Hearing implies obeying. "Faith," Hebrews tells us, "is being certain of what we do not see."

Donald Bloesch, in his book, A Theology of Word & Spirit, observes, "in biblical understanding sight is related to covetousness; what we see we can master and control. Hearing, on the other hand, is associated with faith, for we are wholly dependent on the speaker and our condition is one of waiting rather than strategic planning."

Hearing God speak is essential to faith and to leadership in the church. It is not a picture or visual image that a leader sees and so pursues, but a Word from God that the leader discerns, describes, lives into and invites others to follow.

This is the difference between faith and method; spiritual discovery and marketing. God's design upon a church cannot be defined or measured by numbers or even principles. The goal is not nearly as important as the path. The word "success," as we understand it, is not in God's vocabulary. God is not impressed by our attendance records.

If a vision is not about obtaining goals or success, then what is it for? A vision is the pathway for a dynamic, faith-dependent pursuit of God's will that proves our faithfulness.

Bloesch writes, "In a religion focused on images we become spectators. In a religion oriented about the spoken word we are made active participants." Faith requires action. In our visual-driven culture, relationships are virtual and stories superficial. We say "seeing is believing" because we think visual images persuade most. In fact, they don't. Studies continually demonstrate that people remember more of what they hear than what they see. In hearing, the mind creates its own visual image, influenced by the tone and mood of the voice, communicating far greater emotional impact. Hearing is active. Seeing is passive. Scripture tells us that faith comes by hearing. Luther said, "In order to see God we must learn to stick our eyes in our ears." Jesus said, "The sheep know my voice."

Often at night I would go out to the pasture to check on the sheep. Usually they were grazing some distance away, out of sight and in the dark, ears attentive to any sound of movement. I'd call "sheep! sheep!" in a high pitch voice and as soon as they hear my voice they would come, calling back with loud "baaa's" in return.

Sometimes, when we had guests staying at the house, I would ask a friend to go out with me. I would tell them, "You call the sheep first, like this," and I'd quietly show them how to call. Then they'd try out loud. They would call and call again. The sheep would hear but would not come. Then I would call and the sheep would come running. It is true, sheep know the shepherd's voice.

The voice communicates the relationship. Hearing establishes trust. It is the task of the shepherd leader to hear God's voice, and respond in faith.

Why overseers must be under-hearers.

The Greek word for overseer is derived from the preposition "epi" meaning before or over, and the verb "skopos" meaning "scope" or observe. To oversee, one must know what to look for. This is why it is impossible to embody God's vision without first hearing from Christ. Vision requires audition in order to define and describe the will or standard God is calling us to live into. Here again, we locate ourselves under God's Word. To be overseers we must be under-hearers. Our ability to oversee God's work is directly related to our receptivity to hear and to describe God's voice revealed in Scripture.

But hearing and seeing God's vision is not sufficient. The shepherd leader must live, or embody, the vision. The responsibility is twofold, requiring passion and character. In passion, the shepherd must model the course or goal described. Great is the privilege and responsibility He gives the shepherd-leader to watch over the flock. "Since an overseer is entrusted with God's work, he must be blameless—not overbearing, not quick-tempered, not given to drunkenness, not violent, not pursuing dishonest gain." (Titus 1:7)

God demands honesty and integrity from the shepherd-leader. As the shepherd sees ahead he is entrusted – held accountable – to reach the goal.

Eye on the mark.

When I consult with churches about establishing a vision statement and developing a strategic plan, I recommend that the values, vision and goals be shared. The leadership team needs to guide and facilitate the process, but participation from all levels of the church are invited and welcome.

The big picture is established by leadership listening to God through His people and His Word. But the plans and strategies to achieve the vision are established by those who have to implement and reach the goals.

God gives the vision. Shepherd-leaders keep ears tuned to the Holy Spirit's leading and eyes on the mark, focusing toward the goal.

How leaders embody God's vision

There are four roles for leaders to embody God's vision:

Role one is hearing, and discerning. As we discovered above, a vision is heard before it is seen. We have to hear first from God. Remember: we are casting God's vision, not our own. Vision is not possessed by a leader. It is a gift from God such that the vision possesses the leader. Nor is a vision the sum of majority vote. It is God's vision and it must be heard and obeyed. This requires the ability to listen carefully and to discern rightly. A leader is always asking, "how is God speaking through His Word, His Spirit and His people?" then, "what is God saying?"

Role two is describing. Having heard and discerned, leaders now ask, "what would obedience look like here?" Describe what God is saying in story, words and pictures. Vision must be described before it can be prescribed. To cast the vision, leaders must begin participating in and practicing the vision. If the vision is for evangelism, for example, the leaders must live a passion for the lost. If prayer is a priority, this is demonstrated by leaders on their knees.

Role three is inviting. At every step, members are welcomed into the vision process, invited to join leaders in prayer and study, to seek and discern God's will. (Resistance is directly proportional to involvement.) Having heard, discerned and described, the leader now invites others to follow. Here again, Christ must be center. The invitation is to follow God, not the leader. The leader will focus on Lordship, not event. God's vision is never an event, for instance, building a sanctuary, or a wall. God's vision calls us to deeper worship and relationship. He invites us to Himself, not to Solomon nor Nehemiah.

Role four is proclaiming and encouraging. Nehemiah understood that to complete the wall Israel needed to see God more than a wall. Leaders throughout Scripture remind us of our heritage and encourage perseverance.

When the Apostle Paul was summoned before King Agrippa he

stated his call and conviction emphatically, "I was not disobedient to the vision from heaven." (Acts 26:19) Vision requires persevering obedience.

Embodying a vision must involve communication and action: having a clear statement of what God has called you to do, backed by a life that demonstrates your commitment. (Never recommend any action that you are not already living and committed to complete.)

Paul's vision came through hearing Jesus' voice, and was accompanied by blindness. It was God's call, not what the apostle could foresee. From that time forward, the focus of Paul's life and ministry was never Paul, but God's call to the cross of Christ.

So when division and excess crept into the Corinthian church, the apostle responded firmly and in love, pointing to the cross of Christ, not human words or wisdom.

When John the Baptist was told that there was another, meaning Jesus, who was baptizing, John pointed to Christ, not to himself. "He must become greater, I must become less." Like John the Baptist, the shepherd is the friend of the Bridegroom and his joy is preparing the Bride.

A vision for the church is not a leader's wish list nor dream. A person can only receive what he hears from heaven. The purpose is never to glorify the leader, but to glorify the Bridegroom. The friend waits and "listens." The joy of leading is hearing and following Jesus' voice.

Shepherd leaders must always make Jesus greater and self less. The leader must be "substance building and image reducing," as my friend, John Ryser, says. "God makes leaders from the inside out. Our culture works the other way."

Leaders cast vision through an embodied way of life.

First Church had a clear, compelling vision statement that was widely known and owned by members. Knowing the vision was a strength. Yet the church was facing deep conflict. The evidence of our assessment revealed that First Church leaders failed to embody – that is, to live out – the vision. As a seeker church, First Church was strong in leading people to salvation, but the church had a poor track record of growing up believers into fully committed followers of Jesus Christ.

Most members of First Church measured success by the number of people coming to the seeker service. There was passion for evangelism, but only a vague idea of how to disciple and assimilate new believers into mature faith. Few people spoke about biblical ideals such as holiness, sanctification, and walking with God's Spirit. We found either neglect or great uncertainty as to why or how Christian maturity might happen in the church.

The pastor excelled as an evangelist, but he was not a gifted leader. While he modeled evangelism he neglected discipleship. The church followed his lead.

The result was a church that was pre-occupied with a model of ministry that emphasized one ideal at the expense of another, creating a series of unintended negative consequences that threatened the future of the church. While seekers came through the front door, mature Christians were leaving through the back. The vision statement was committed to evangelism and discipleship but leaders were failing to embody the latter while being one dimensional in its approach to the former.

As mature believers left the church frustrated, new believers and non-believers were pressed into service. Without the required training, experience or maturity, they soon failed or became frustrated. Assimilation meant becoming involved in a ministry rather than being discipled into the spiritual growth of the church. The pattern became "get in" (conversion), "get busy" (usually in a ministry supporting getting others in), then "get out" (leaving bewildered or seeking more spiritual growth).

When mature believers voiced concern that discipleship was being short-changed and evangelism was too often limited to a weekly event, they were criticized for a "lack of commitment or involvement." The greater issue was the lack of leadership in embodying a comprehensive discipleship, mentoring, and equipping plan that empowered and released people into the full life of the church.

We should never confuse the gifts of administration with leadership. While both are general functions of leadership, the gift of leadership is distinct in nature and form from managing or administering people. In fact, good leaders are often not good managers or administrators. Men and women with the gift of leadership think and act very differently.

Leaders are visionaries who see the big picture, envision great goals and inspire bold work. They set the "why," not the "how" of a church's direction. Gifted leaders are spiritual entrepreneurs. They are risk-takers and motivators. A compelling vision needs a gifted leader for two reasons: (1) to ensure the vision is bold and compelling (usually picturing a result beyond present comfort and ability) and (2) to help motivate others to have the faith and confidence in Christ to embody the vision.

Every church must have at least one leader serving this role. Since all church leadership should involve a team, the visionary leadership role does not have to be the senior pastor. Of course, this requires a willingness of the pastor to recognize and empower others.

Chapter Four Review:

In this chapter we looked at the second of seven tasks every leader must always do. Meet with your leadership team to complete and discuss the following exercise. Read each statement. Using the scale provided, indicate how true each statement is for your leadership team. Indicate how you really feel (not what you think you ought to.) Ask yourself: "Does this statement describe our actual habits and practices?"

If the statement is always true, place the number 5 on the line in front of the statement. If the statement is never true, then write the number 0 on the line. Place the number (0-5) that is the most accurate description of your actual leadership practice.

SCALE
5 = Always true.
4 = Often true.
3 = Sometimes true.
2 = Seldom true.
1 = Almost never true.
0 = Never true.

Please answer these statements referring to your actual practice. Be honest. Don't hesitate to choose a 5 or 0. Avoid using 3.

Embodying God's vision:

6) _____ We often set apart time to listen to God's voice and to discern His will through Scripture study and prayer.

7) _____ We have heard a compelling call (of what God is saying to us), and have seen a clear picture of where God is leading us.

8) _____ Most people in our church know and own God's vision for our church.

9) _____ We (leaders and members) are moving together in the same direction.

10) _____ Our actions (as leaders) demonstrate our passion for our vision.

Compare and discuss your responses, asking questions such as:

"Why? What is it about us that we are thinking or acting this way?"

"What is God saying to us that we need to hear?"

"How long has this been true about us?" or "When did this start?"

"What would we need to do to address these results?"

Chapter Five:
Defining Current Reality

The LORD sent Nathan to David. When he came to him,
he said, "There were two men in a certain town, one rich and the
other poor. The rich man had a very large number of sheep and cattle,
but the poor man had nothing except one little ewe lamb he had
bought. He raised it, and it grew up with him and his children.
It shared his food, drank from his cup and even slept in his arms.
It was like a daughter to him. "Now a traveler came to the rich
man, but the rich man refrained from taking one of his own sheep
or cattle to prepare a meal for the traveler who had come to him.
Instead, he took the ewe lamb that belonged to the poor man and
prepared it for the one who had come to him." David burned with
anger against the man and said to Nathan, "As surely as the LORD
lives, the man who did this deserves to die! He must pay for that lamb
four times over, because he did such a thing and had no pity."
Then Nathan said to David, "You are the man! 2 Samuel 12: 1-7

Imagine drawing Nathan's assignment to go confront King David about his sin. Think of Moses, Esther, John the Baptist and others who God called upon at strategic times to bring a word of rebuke.

Speaking the truth when the truth is hard or unpleasant to face is a task many leaders avoid and few handle well. Part of the failure can be explained by skill. A person who is not a leader is often unskilled confronting sin, correcting failure or saying hard things. It is hard to be the bearer of bad news. Further, there is a long tradition of God's people killing prophets. However, the same tradition has otherwise weak people rise up to speak God's truth with boldness.

Defining current reality is the first step to speaking the truth in love. It means identifying, discerning, then saying directly and lovingly what is.

We served a church where the former pastor was remembered as a superhero. He came to the church when there was just a handful of older members. Three years later the church was filled with vibrant young families and new believers. The youth group was active and more than 250 children came through the VBS program every summer. This pastor was a wonderful loving person. He was involved in the Kiwanis Club, coached the high school soccer team, was active in the community, directed the church youth group, lead Bible studies and preached. Everything the church did, this pastor was behind.

No progress comes without cost. In the same time the church grew from 10 to 250, the pastor's marriage fell apart. Within four years he was separated, divorced and stepping over boundaries with several women in the church.

When the pastor resigned, the church fell from its own weight. The youth group disbanded, people split into factions and many left the church. When we were called in, we found a divided church membership battling over the legacy and future direction of the church. For some the former pastor was a hero, for others, someone they wanted to forget.

The first group wanted to forgive and forget his marital problems and ignore the charges brought by women deeply wounded by the pastor's indiscretions. The other group was glad to have him out but did not want to say why.

No one wanted to face the truth: that their pastor was a gifted evangelist with deep character flaws. Further, few could see how the church was part of the problem. By allowing the pastor to build the church at the expense of his family, church members and leaders failed the pastor.

Few issues in the church are as bad as they appear or as good as you want them to be. A leader must tell it like it is. "This is God's vision for the church, or marriage, or discipleship," a pastor must explain, "and we are not there." It is never loving to ignore or bend the truth in favor of protecting feelings. Proverbs 27: 5-6 tells us, "Better is open rebuke than hidden love. Wounds from a friend can be trusted, but an enemy multiplies kisses."

To define current reality, a leader must be willing to acknowledge and confess weaknesses as well as celebrate strengths; to expose sin as well as proclaim forgiveness. Thus, defining current reality is the truthful description of what is, measured against what was and will be.

Let's take a closer look at several key words in this definition to understand, and to apply, what this means for your church.

On being truthful

Defining current reality requires a truthful assessment of what is –

an unbiased and unvarnished statement about reality. There are at least two requirements for being truthful:

1) Discerning what is true, and
2) Confessing the truth discerned.

Defining reality requires discernment. Discernment starts by asking, "what is God saying?" To answer this question accurately, one must learn to listen and to think biblically. Jesus said "By their fruit you will recognize them." When something is wrong, but you are not sure what or why, here is a simple rule: always follow the fruit. In Galatians, Paul describes good and bad fruit. People who are not walking with God's Spirit are tainted by sexual immorality, greed, hatred, discord, fits of rage, jealousy and selfishness. Find these in someone and you know they are not walking closely with God. But if you find joy, peace, patience and so on, those are the marks of spiritual growth.

Every farmer knows that fruit takes time to grow. A leader walking with God's Spirit will evidence spiritual fruit. A leader does not, for instance, decide to embezzle funds or commit adultery overnight. Rather the seed takes root in hundreds of small concessions and steps in the wrong direction. (That is why the Apostle Paul urges all believers to keep in step and to sow continually to the Spirit.) In time, the seed sown bears fruit, but there are always signs before the fruit.

Discerning the fruit of words, actions and decisions may be complex and oftentimes subtle, but there are always signs. It is the function of spiritual leadership to "keep watch" and to recognize the signs in people as we would look for the flower and fruit of a plant.

Jesus says, "Remain in me, and I will remain in you. No branch can bear fruit by itself; it must remain in the vine. Neither can you bear fruit unless you remain in me. "I am the vine; you are the branches. If a man remains in me and I in him, he will bear much fruit; apart from me you can do nothing." (John 15:4,5)

Being truthful starts with discernment and leads to confession. The truth rightly discerned must be lovingly spoken. To be truthful one can neither minimize the negative, nor overstate the positive. Here again, we face immediate obstacles brought forward by faulty assumptions. Many in the church today resist speaking the truth about difficult matters for fear of hurting others. Some go so far as to say that stating weakness gives power to it. Scripture affirms the opposite, "Better is open rebuke than hidden love," says Solomon. "Wounds from a friend can be trusted, but an enemy multiplies kisses." (Proverbs 27: 5-6)

Defining current reality means speaking the truth in love about what is – the present condition of the church. It is directly related to embodying God's vision. Reality offers leaders the opportunity to re-state and motivate people toward God's vision. A leader must be able to say clearly, "Here is God's vision. We are not there." The danger in keeping silent about reality is that people are lulled into believing what is, is all there is.

We have seen this frequently in churches who proudly proclaim values of tolerance and acceptance in order to attract unbelievers, such as "all are welcome here" and "come as you are." Again, what has great appeal in Western democracy has little to do with biblical Christianity. In many of these open-minded churches we find people who come as they are and stay as they are. Many profess faith, but their marriages, child raising and habits of behavior show no demonstrable difference from people who are, for instance, good citizens.

Defining current reality recognizes the truth that God has called the church to be a living witness to the transforming power of the cross; to live such lives that our living stands in stark contrast to the world around us, namely that we are "a chosen people, a royal priesthood, a holy nation, a people belonging to God," and this, so that the church "may declare the praises of him who called you out of darkness into his wonderful light." (1Peter 2: 9)

Peter goes on to exhort his readers, "I urge you, as aliens and strangers in the world, to abstain from sinful desires, which war against your soul. Live such good lives among the pagans that, though they accuse you of doing wrong, they may see your good deeds and glorify God on the day he visits us." (1Peter 2:11-12) This echoes Paul's words to the Ephesians, "I urge you to live a life worthy of the calling you have received." (Ephesians 4:1)

Paul and Peter are speaking about fruit, not accomplishment. Defining current reality is about the spiritual result of a vision – its embodiment in changed lives. Leadership must be clear about what really is true and what merely appears to be so. They must go beyond quantity (how many) to ask what kind of fruit is being produced.

Description of what is

The Holy Scriptures announce a radical, upside-down Kingdom. This Kingdom is radical because it heralds a way of hearing, seeing and acting based upon the life, death and resurrection of Jesus, the Messiah King. This Kingdom is upside-down because the Son of God becomes the Son of Man, the King becomes suffering Servant, the Shepherd becomes sacrificial Lamb.

To live faithfully into the story of Jesus, one must describe a reality that is past, present and future, both immediate and eternal. In a world clamoring for instant gratification of personal needs, the Gospel proclaims a new community based upon a historic tradition, awaiting a future hope. We are not yet what we were called and are being made to be. We are, as Peter wrote, "aliens and strangers" living by faith for the return of Christ, not individuals seeking the fulfillment of personal needs. To be Christian means to say with Paul "to live is Christ and to die is gain." The reality of the Gospel is a Kingdom established in the past, present, and yet to come.

What was and will be

No person knows God's plan or truth completely. God is omniscient, we see only in part. Faith is about obedience, not a sure bet. This requires a specific way of seeing – a perspective that is both eternal and immediate. Before the Creation of the world, God knew us and chose us to be "holy and blameless." To God, a day is as a thousand years. Yet God says "Today, if you hear my voice, do not harden your hearts." Scripture instructs leaders to measure current reality by God's Promises of the past and Hope for the future. To do this requires a long view and a daily approach.

The long view. First, we must see the church in light of God's eternal plan. God's purpose must come prior to and woven into every thought and action, like a book that is being written whose Author already knows the outcome. On the one hand, this eternal perspective requires spiritual memory – the ability to accurately remember God's redemptive acts through history. In Scripture, remembering is often linked with repentance (See Rev. 2:5;3:3). We remember what was promised and received and we see how far we have fallen. On the other hand, an eternal perspective calls for anticipating what will be. The apostle Paul writes, "Not that I have already obtained all this, or have already been made perfect, but I press on to take hold of that for which Christ Jesus took hold of me." (Philippians 3:12) For Paul, present reality is guided by a future hope.

The Church embodies God's narrative of faith. This faith looks both backward to tradition and forward to consummation. It looks backward through the millenniums of God's active, faithful work in the life of His people, and forward to the completion of history when His Bride will be presented perfect before the Father. It is here we stand in the continuum of faith, seeking God's face, listening for His voice, and defining current reality. Such a perspective tells us what is important and what is trivial, what is temporary and what is eternal. As the apostle Paul tells us, "His intent was that now, through the church, the manifold wisdom of God should be made known to the rulers and authorities in the heavenly realms, according to his eternal purpose which he accomplished in Christ Jesus our Lord." (Ephesians 3:10-11)

A daily approach. Yet God meets us daily. God provided manna each morning for the Israelites wandering in the wilderness. The psalmist exhorts, "This is the day the Lord has made, let us rejoice in it and be glad." Paul writes, "Inwardly we are being renewed day by day."

The God of all history is faithful and active in everyday life, and in day-by-day ministry. He is concerned with our afflictions, and provides perspective to our "light" and momentary troubles. The spiritual leader will see God today, His hand in the work He gives now, measured in light of His eternal plan. We are to pray with the disciples, "give us this day our daily bread." The church is called to faithfully participate in God's redemptive plan, and to put on display a life that is possible only through the life, death and resurrection of Jesus.

These twin perspectives - a long view and a daily approach - will help the shepherd leader discern, define and describe faithfulness in time of decision, conflict or uncertainty.

Our current reality

A common mistake leaders make in failing to define current reality is to look at events, rather than patterns, and to quantify results rather than to discern fruit. This is the difference between methodology and ecclesiology. Methodology is about doing. It is temporal and rooted in human "works." Ecclesiology is about being. It is founded in a forever Kingdom initiated and completed by God's grace. Much conflict and failure arises in the church when leaders use human methods to achieve divine purposes.

Methods will always fail because they assume the values of individualism and standards of human performance that stand in opposition to spiritual faithfulness. The problem is that our thinking is so diseased that we call this failure "success." To notice this, one could simply examine the leadership section in Christian bookstores or the "how to" subjects of church leadership conferences. Instead of a dynamically interconnected, living organism motivated and sustained by God's Spirit, the church has become a product to be sold, or a machine to be fixed by experts. For example, the vision-building process advocated by most church consultants does not include waiting before the Lord in common prayer and Scripture study, but begins and ends with "results."

The logic for this transactional, result oriented thinking is twofold: 1) that the church is competing against popular media and entertainment for the hearts and minds of people, and that therefore 2) the church must use every method and tool of culture to proclaim the Gospel. This rationale makes great sense to marketers and consumers. After all, a works theology works! Yet, to start here is to forget that the Church is a living organism, not a product; it is a called out, called together community of righteousness that bears witness to eternal, not human purposes and powers.

A preoccupation with "what works" will always lead to human-centered leadership and human centered leadership will inevitably result in coercion and human manipulation. It does so because experience and expertise is the prime mover behind methods. We speak of God's will and leading but we secretly believe and not so secretly exalt the eloquent speaker, innovative leader and charismatic personality who makes things happen.

Contrast these ideals to Scripture where God chooses the least and the weakest to build his Kingdom. Biblical leadership is always about faithfulness, not human methods and power.

Therefore, questions such as "what does God want me/us to do?" or "how can we be more successful?" will always lead down the wrong path because questions like these assume that God's work is separate (or even in competition) from one church to another. God's purpose is never divided. Instead, Scripture teaches us to ask, "What is God's purpose and activity in our world?" Leadership grounded in ecclesiology instead of methodology will seek to know, discern and faithfully act in cooperation with God's Spirit. God alone is object and subject. His work is always about Him, never about us. This requires a deep understanding of God's purposes that both precede and follow after us. Our concern here is to ensure that we think biblically so that our discernment is not sabotaged or manipulated by a works theology.

As we travel around the nation speaking to leaders and working with churches in conflict we find leaders struggling to discern and to speak the truth about the nature and function of the church. Leaders have allowed personal failure and hurt, in themselves and others, to privatize faith. Rights and privacy keep leaders from acknowledging failure and confessing sin in themselves while overlooking patterns of sin in others. Oddly, this individualism is also keeping the church from celebrating and remembering God's saving work in history.

In short, many church leaders are managing, not leading the church. Caught up in the latest technique for attracting interest or meeting needs, they are unwittingly (for most leaders would be horrified to see themselves this way) following a "works" theology – that God plus our innovation, methods and appeal will convince the masses. This is dangerous in obvious and subtle ways exactly because "works" will "work" in the short-run, (if by "working" one measures attendance, excitement and so on) but rarely produces fruit that will last.

So, the question is not "what works?" but "what kind of fruit are our works producing?" I'm fearful that the fruit of some efforts are training people how to be consumer Christians – to think and to act as individuals who now find in Jesus another way to meet their needs, or to get what they want. The problem, of course, is that our story has a cross.

As we ask God to help us see ourselves truthfully, we need to ask hard questions, such as: What are we saving people into? Are we truly forming followers of Jesus, the Messiah King? Are lives being transformed such that the fruit of our collective life – our mutual submission, fellowship and worship – as well as our marriages, child-raising and relationships bear witness to the powers of the resurrected Christ?

To define current reality we must speak the truth in love.

Chapter Five Review:

In this chapter we looked at the third of seven tasks every leader must always do. Meet with your leadership team to complete and discuss the following exercise. Read each statement. Using the scale provided, indicate how true each statement is for your leadership team. Indicate how you really feel (not what you think you ought to.) Ask yourself: "Does this statement describe our actual habits and practices?"

If the statement is always true, place the number 5 on the line in front of the statement. If the statement is never true, then write the number 0 on the line. Place the number (0-5) that is the most accurate description of your actual leadership practice.

SCALE
5 = Always true.
4 = Often true.
3 = Sometimes true.
2 = Seldom true.
1 = Almost never true.
0 = Never true.

Please answer these statements referring to your actual practice. Be honest. Don't hesitate to choose a 5 or 0. Avoid using 3.

Defining current reality:
11) _____ We openly speak about our strengths and weaknesses.
12) _____ We make and keep measurable goals.
13) _____ We regularly evaluate our progress and identify problems to address.
14) _____ We resolve conflict openly, directly and redemptively.
15) _____ We have open, honest and free communication of ideas and disagreements in leadership.

Compare and discuss your responses, asking questions such as:

"Why? What is it about us that we are thinking or acting this way?"

"What is God saying to us that we need to hear?"

—

"How long has this been true about us?" or "When did this start?"

"What would we need to do to address these results?"

Chapter Six:
Setting and Keeping Boundaries

*Keep watch over yourselves and all the flock of which the Holy Spirit
has made you overseers. Be shepherds of the church of God,
which he bought with his own blood. Acts 20:28*

Every Christmas our family bought a new jigsaw puzzle to put
together. It was a family tradition for many years (up until the year we
discovered that none of us ever really liked jigsaw puzzles.)

To start, of course, we opened the box, dumped out the pieces and
turned all of them right-side up. Then we propped up the box cover so
we could see the design and refer back to it constantly as we slowly put
the pieces together. The only thing I liked about putting together the
puzzle was the start. It was my job to find and to join all the straight
edges that framed the puzzle. After this I usually said, "the rest is up to
you."

This, in a way of speaking, is what every leader must do. Imagine
the church as the puzzle and the scene – say a mountain landscape or a
city skyline – as the vision. The leader frames the boundary and keeps
pointing to the box cover to remind and encourage others about what the
finished scene will look like. Each member, to continue the analogy, is
an interlocking piece of the puzzle, all of which are necessary to
complete the scene.

Shepherds set and keep boundaries because sheep are prone to
wander. The word "sheep" translated in the New Testament has the same
Greek root for our English word "probation." The word is "probaton,"
derived from the prefix "pro" meaning "before", and "basis" meaning "a
stepping or walking." The word literally means "before walking" or
"before stepping out."

When Scripture refers to the church as a flock and to God's people
as sheep, the Holy Spirit is saying that we – all of us – are "on probation."

To be on probation means that we have the present capability, and past culpability, of doing wrong. We may choose to follow Christ or go astray. This assumes a former waywardness. We were lost, but God found us. The question is not whether we are guilty or fallen. We are. All of us, like sheep, have gone astray. The question is will we turn and follow Christ?

Herding is a natural instinct of sheep. Their strength and protection is being together.

One summer we had a violent thunderstorm move through our area. The wind, hail, thunder and lightning were powerful and frightening. I was concerned about the sheep so I took a flashlight and headed into the pasture. A tree had fallen on their shelter and the sheep bolted in fright. Calling "sheep" in a loud voice I heard them answer, baaing from the back corner of the pasture. All the ewes and lambs were huddled together in the rain. Calling again, the sheep came running to me as one, back to the protection of the shelter.

The Apostle Peter says "you were like sheep going astray, but now you have returned to the Shepherd and Overseer of your souls." The context here, as in most of Scripture is not individual sheep but the flock, the church.

Leaders will do well to remember their status as sheep as well as their calling as shepherds before God. You will lead others to the extent you are following Christ. That is why Paul exhorts the Ephesian elders to "Keep watch over yourselves and all the flock of which the Holy Spirit has made you overseers. Be shepherds of the church of God, which he bought with his own blood," (Acts 20:28) and why he warns the Galatian church to "watch yourself, or you also may be tempted." (Gal 6:1)

Every Spring, when we had sheep, we walked the fence line of our property before putting the sheep out to pasture. If there was a hole in the fence, we would mend it. Otherwise, the sheep would find the hole and wander through. When one sheep finds a way out, all the sheep will follow.

People are the same. "We all, like sheep, have gone astray, each of us has turned to his own way; and the LORD has laid on him the iniquity of us all." (Is. 53:6) There is something about us that wants to know and test boundaries.

A primary role of the shepherd-leader is to set and keep boundaries.

Boundaries are needed for who you are, what you value and how you serve. Here, again, we are helped by having a clear vision and compelling purpose. A good vision tells you what you should not be doing as well as what you should.

Setting boundaries through goals.

Goals are boundaries that focus and motivate people as well as keep them from harm. Goals are one tangible way to provide direction, keep focus and to measure faithfulness in a church. Just as "audition" establishes vision, so the vision will establish direction and goals that will serve as guideposts, or boundaries for fulfilling the vision. There is a spiritual imperative for goals. The Greek word "planao" meaning "to go astray" figuratively means "the absence of a goal." Without goals, sheep will wander. Without a vision, a pastor leads sheep astray.

Consider Abraham, Moses, Gideon and Paul, for example. God gave each man a vision with a goal. To Abraham he said, "leave your country and go to the land I will show you." Later God revealed His plan to make a nation from Abraham's seed. Moses is called to tell Pharaoh to "let my people go," to deliver Israel out of slavery. Gideon was called to battle, to save Israel from Midian's hand. Paul was called to be a servant in order that the Gospel would be taken to the Gentiles.

A vision is not a goal. Goals spring from and follow after vision. Goals are the steps of faith to fulfill the vision.

While God gives the "what" and "why," Scripture seems to allow great latitude with "how." It is in the "how" that we prove our faith and understand God's will. God leads as we follow.

Abraham was willing to offer Isaac even though it contradicted all of what God had promised. Abraham obeyed, assuming God would raise Isaac from the dead. Moses did not know how God would deliver Israel from Egypt, only that He would. Gideon was led to reduce his fighting force, an absurd idea for making war. Paul constantly writes of wanting to visit churches, but for one reason or another God kept him from doing so.

Obedience, not knowing ahead how God will work, is the key to faith and leading. It is our ability to hope against hope, not calculate the odds, that God desires. In the church obedience follows common prayer, common study and common life.

Scripture refers to sin as a "missing the mark" or failing to reach a goal. To lead, one must faithfully keep the boundaries that are set.

Boundaries and discipline

The writer to the Hebrews writes, *My son, do not make light of the*

Lord's discipline, and do not lose heart when he rebukes you, because the Lord disciplines those he loves, and he punishes everyone he accepts as a son. Endure hardship as discipline; God is treating you as sons. For what son is not disciplined by his father? If you are not disciplined (and everyone undergoes discipline), then you are illegitimate children and not true sons. Moreover, we have all had human fathers who disciplined us and we respected them for it. How much more should we submit to the Father of our spirits and live! Our fathers disciplined us for a little while as they thought best; but God disciplines us for our good, that we may share in his holiness. No discipline seems pleasant at the time, but painful. Later on, however, it produces a harvest of righteousness and peace for those who have been trained by it. (Hebrews 12:5b-11)

Setting boundaries requires keeping boundaries. The expectation is that when boundaries are crossed, action must be taken in a loving, non-coercive way. Here is where the true heart of leadership is tested, and where most leaders fail. Discipline in never about punishment. Discipline is always about restoration – restoring a sinner to fellowship with God and with one another.

Scripture gives clear instructions for holy living. God promises to bless obedience and to judge sin. The Bible is the story of God working justice and righteousness in light of man's rebellion. However, Church history is marked by human attempts to interpret and enforce God's commands, often erring at the extremes – from legalism to subjectivism. The challenge for a biblical community is to discern what is the nature and function of godly life. Like parents with children, leaders must engage parishioners to common study and agreement about:

Expectations & Descriptions: what it means to be holy and what this would look like in the context of our life together – offering reasonable and clearly understood guidelines and descriptions for people to follow.

Responsibilities: the church must agree about the role of leaders, parents and church members to offer compassionate and consistent encouragement and correction – granting freedom of form, while giving permission for brothers and sisters in Christ to come alongside in loving rebuke, correction and encouragement.

Here, again, we find that biblical leadership is primarily about discernment, description and invitation, not methodology. To rebuke, correct and encourage requires a way of thinking biblically and acting spiritually – a way of interpreting and describing. Yet this is not acknowledged or addressed in most churches and, when it is addressed, often falls into one of two extremes: rule-based legalism, or emotion-driven relativism.

Scripture challenges the leader to think and to act like Jesus. This means we need to interpret and address boundaries in a way that would allow for such divergent responses as:

1. Jesus rebuking the Pharisees harshly ("woe to you"), and for Paul to direct the Corinthians to "cast the sinner out" while at the same time permitting
2. Jesus saying to the woman caught in adultery "neither do I condemn you, go and sin no more."

Methods, rules and how-to's simply cannot supply the discernment necessary to make these judgments. Spiritual boundaries can never be mere laws or rules. To make them so inevitably results in a works not grace-based community. Grace implies and requires spiritual discernment. How is this possible?

Binding and loosing

In his excellent essay *Binding And Loosing*, (The Royal Priesthood, Herald Press 1998), John Howard Yoder observes that Jesus uses the word "church" only two times, and each time he does so in connection to binding and loosing. But, what does it mean to bind and to loose? What is this power given to the church?

Yoder offers a twofold meaning. First, binding and loosing is about forgiveness. To "bind" is to withhold fellowship, to "loose" is to forgive. The church is given the extraordinary, even scandalous, responsibility to pronounce forgiveness and restore broken fellowship in Jesus' name. It is scandalous because "forgiving sins" was what got Jesus in the most trouble with the Pharisees. "Who can forgive but God?" It is extraordinary because this same responsibility is given to the church.

That is why, second, Yoder says binding and loosing requires discernment. To bind is to forbid or make obligatory; to "loose" is to leave free or permit. In order to render forgiveness, the church must discern and keep the boundaries of fellowship, (i.e., how we are to live together under the Lordship of Jesus Christ.) Forgiving presupposes discernment. At the same time, discernment necessitates forgiveness. Each depend completely on leaders seeking out and keeping step with God's Spirit.

We recently served a church where a new senior pastor was accused of an inappropriate relationship with a woman from his previous church.

At first the pastor denied the relationship, seeking to cover up; then he admitted the "mistake" but minimized his responsibility, claiming it was the woman who was stalking him.

The elders of the church quickly split over the issue. Some elders defended the pastor, believing he was repentant. The church, they proposed, should forgive the pastor immediately and quickly restore him to ministry. Other elders felt that the pastor did not demonstrate brokenness and was not taking full responsibility for his sin. The first group of elders accused the others of being unforgiving and legalistic while the latter accused the former of relativism. Deadlocked in this disagreement, the church cycled into deep conflict, dividing the church. People were forced to take sides with the elders for or against the pastor. After nine months, the pastor resigned under a cloud of confusion and many members left the church in protest.

This scenario, or one like it, is repeated in hundreds of churches every year because leaders fail to understand and practice binding and loosing – biblical forgiveness and discernment.

The elders in the church mentioned above failed because they allowed their disagreement to become the issue rather than the fruit of the pastor's life. Some elders wanted to "loose" (to forgive) without discernment. They chose to trust the pastor's account without checking his claims. The other elders wanted to "bind" because of their discernment, but did so as prosecutors, not in loving restoration. In the end, we found that the pastor had repeatedly lied and manipulated the process. He had a history of doing so from the church he served previously, (a reference the search committee had neglected to check.)

Setting and keeping boundaries in discipline requires leaders who discern before they forgive and, in forgiving, discern how boundaries provide opportunities for grace.

Yoder makes four critical points regarding authority and binding & loosing:

1. The authority given to the church to forgive is parallel to the authority of Jesus Christ. (John 20:20)
2. This forgiveness is costly.
3. The church is empowered to bind and loose in Jesus' Name by the Holy Spirit. (John 14:16)
4. In binding and loosing the church becomes the Church. (Mat 16:18; 18:15-17)

The keys to kingdom cannot be found anywhere else in the world.

When a church does not practice or live in biblical discernment and forgiveness, it forfeits the transforming power of the cross.

Boundaries and counseling

In our experience working with pastors and leaders who have committed adultery or sexual sin, most cases involved a failure to set and keep boundaries while counseling someone of the opposite sex.

Pastoral counseling is hazardous ground for pastor and church alike and must be considered with great caution. There are three reasons to be wary.

First, a leader who counsels many hours a week will, by necessity, spend the majority of time with the weakest and most chronically dependent members of the church – the one lost sheep, instead of the ninety-nine. A shepherd spending time with the weakest sheep will be at the rear, not in front of the flock. A shepherd must lead from the front.

Second, the church gathered, not the pastor alone, is where personal needs must be met. The church is called first and foremost to be a vital, growing community, a people ministering to one another. The church that operates as a true biblical community offers hurting people a safe place to openly share their sorrows, faults and frustrations, without fear of judgment or gossip. Such churches place the responsibility for nurture and growth in the Body of Christ, not in a professional clergy.

The third reason why counseling is harmful to leader and church is the threat to overstepping emotional, sexual and even spiritual boundaries. Boundary keeping assumes and requires a community where the basis for giving and receiving counsel is a common fellowship and commitment to the Lordship of Christ.

Boundaries give freedom for brothers and sisters to live into the family of God.

Chapter Six Review:

In this chapter we looked at the fourth of seven tasks every leader must always do. Meet with your leadership team to complete and discuss the following exercise. Read each statement. Using the scale provided, indicate how true each statement is for your leadership team. Indicate how you really feel (not what you think you ought to.) Ask yourself: "Does this statement describe our actual habits and practices?"

If the statement is always true, place the number 5 on the line in front of the statement. If the statement is never true, then write the number 0 on the line. Place the number (0-5) that is the most accurate description of your actual leadership practice.

SCALE
5 = Always true.
4 = Often true.
3 = Sometimes true.
2 = Seldom true.
1 = Almost never true.
0 = Never true.

Please answer these statements referring to your actual practice. Be honest. Don't hesitate to choose a 5 or 0. Avoid using 3.

Setting and keeping boundaries:
16) _____ We make decisions guided by our vision.
17) _____ We keep the decisions we make. (We keep our promises.)
18) _____ When boundaries are challenged, we speak the truth in love to correct, rebuke and encourage.
19) _____ We conduct effective, efficient meetings.
20) _____ We manage standard details well; complete assignments on time.

Compare and discuss your responses, asking questions such as:

"Why? What is it about us that we are thinking or acting this way?"

"What is God saying to us that we need to hear?"

"How long has this been true about us?" or "When did this start?"

"What would we need to do to address these results?"

Chapter Seven:
Feeding and Nurturing the Flock

I am the good shepherd; I know my sheep and my sheep know me.
John 10:14

In the New Testament, the Greek root word for shepherd means to feed, to rule and nourish. A pastor is called to guide and nurture the flock.

One summer years ago we experienced an extended drought in New England. While the Midwest was flooded, the East was bone dry. This became a problem on our farm. We have only six acres of pasture area to accommodate up to 20 sheep. To keep both sheep and pastures healthy, we rotate the animals between two pastures, keeping the animals feeding in one pasture while the other has time to grow. As dry weather slows the field's growing, our sheep do not slow their eating.

As the summer wore on, our pastures withered. Typically, sheep will rest during the day and graze during the cool of night. Each pasture, being a pasture, is clear of trees. There was little shade, except for a line of towering maples bordering the brook running through our property. Our sheep were in the habit of laying down along the fence at the top of the pasture fully exposed to the heat of the day. There they lay in their wool sweaters all day long, panting. Toward the end of the summer we had another particularly hot spell.

One blazing hot afternoon I looked out at our panting sheep and decided we should have a little talk. "You know," I said quietly approaching the sheep laying along the fence line, "it would be a lot cooler if you girls went down to the brook." The sheep listened respect-fully, even if they could not understand a word. They stared back at me, twitching their ears and chewing their cud.

We have to change our notion of a pastor from that of a teacher preacher to a shepherd leader. Preaching and teaching are vital. Christ commissions his disciples to preach the Gospel. Paul admonishes elders to teach, and reserves a special honor for those who teach and preach (1 Tim 5:17). But teaching and preaching do not equal shepherding and should not be considered so. Rather teaching and preaching must serve the greater need to lead and feed.

On that hot summer day with my sheep panting under the sun, I learned a lesson about teaching. I quit talking to the sheep and hopped over the fence, then walked down to the brook ahead of the sheep, calling them by name. The sheep followed. When I sat down in the shade, they grazed for awhile and laid down also – by the cool stream.

From that day forward, my sheep always rested during the heat of the day in the same place by the brook. There is no persuasion like discovery.

We are not called to know facts about God, but to know Him. Knowing things about God is not knowing God. Christianity is not the sum total of what we know about God, nor what we imagine Him to be, but Who God is and how His character confronts and changes our life, our very being.

Leaders are not called merely to present the Living Water but to drink deeply from it and welcome others to join in their discovery. A leader brings people to the "river whose streams make glad the city of God." (Psalm 46: 4)

A well-worn path.

Sitting on our back porch overlooking the pasture with the brook running through, you will see lush green grass growing everywhere except a well worn dirt path that leads down the hillside to the brook. It is the path of discovery, the path my sheep have now taken for water hundreds and thousands of times.

In the New Testament, Christians are called people of the Way. The word for Way literally means a well-worn path. A leader's task is to introduce the flock to the One who is the Way, Truth and Life by leading them down the path of discovery. This means, a leader cannot merely point the way. He must leave the pulpit and leave the committee meetings and enter into the everyday lives of people to show the way.

A leader who does not lead by example raises a flock who will listen politely but never move. The leader's task is to provide pasture, it falls to the sheep to eat and drink. The sheep must feed themselves. They must taste the lush green grass and swallow the cool clear water. To paraphrase an old line, a shepherd can lead the sheep to pasture and water, but he cannot make them eat and drink.

First milk.

Once, when one of my older ewes had twins, her milk did not come in. This presented an emergency. Without a mother's first milk lambs are susceptible to disease and can become sick or even die within hours. First milk is called colostrum, a remarkable natural concoction packed with all the anti-bodies and nutrients a newborn needs for fighting off parasites and disease – in humans, cows, sheep and every mammal. After a quick call to Hans, the dairy farmer who lives up the road, we soon had a bottle of cow colostrum, kept in the refrigerator for just such emergencies.

With colostrum warmed on the stove and poured into bottles fitted with nipples we hand fed the lambs every two hours around the clock for the next week. Mercifully, our ewe's milk finally came in and we let nature run its good course. Soon, we added high protein grain to the lamb's diet by means of a creep feed, an enclosed space lambs can enter to eat all they want, but ewes cannot enter because of the size of the doors and openings. The lambs learned to eat the grain by mimicking the older sheep. In four months the lambs were large and strong, completely weaned and able to graze openly with the other sheep in the pasture. Within a year these lambs, now yearlings, were bred to have lambs of their own.

The shepherd's role in the nurture and growth of a lamb mirrors the role of a leader in a church. We call it discipleship. It is the task of leadership to provide the spiritual colostrum and sustenance that new believers crave in order to grow.

Dependency may be necessary for a time, but the leader's task is always to equip believers to feed themselves. To feed and nourish the flock, a leader must guide people from first milk to solid food.

Leaders who are learners, not knowers.

The tendency of many leaders, like most other people, is to stay within comfort zones – close to what they know and far from what they have yet to master or learn.

We are programmed to think this way. Most of us were taught to think in linear, cause and effect, objective ways. We thrive on scientific proof – of knowing facts, doctrines and truth. We show less interest in discovering the unknown or even practicing what we learn.

Leaders who are knowers and not learners are reluctant to enter fully into the life of the church, remaining outside and above it. This fosters both a perception and the reality of the pastor being detached and removed – one who knows things but who is unknown. As we saw above, shepherding requires trust and trust requires relationship. A leader must enter into shared discovery in order to lead a congregation.

Stanley Hauerwas, in his article "Discipleship as a craft, Church as a disciplined Community" offers helpful insight about our need to be trained. "Christian life is not voluntary," Hauerwas states. "You cannot become a Christian without training." We might say the same for leadership.

By training, Hauerwas means the formation of the self through participation in and submission to the Church, what he calls a "disciplined community." We must learn holiness as a craft, in the same way an apprentice bricklayer might learn to lay brick. "It is not sufficient to be told how to do it; you must learn to mix the mortar, use a trowel and so on," Hauerwas states.

Discipleship is like brick-laying. In order to lay brick you must "hour after hour day after day, lay brick." To be a disciple you must take up the cross daily. Church members need a pastor who will show them, day by day, what it means to follow Jesus, not merely tell them once a week. In order to train others a pastor must be learning also. This is not an isolated or individual act. Neither pastor nor bricklayer can simply go away to conferences or shut himself up in the study. There is no learning without practice. Pastors who learn with their people are better able to teach and lead them.

As Hauerwas reminds us, to learn to lay brick is to be initiated into a history, a culture and a language of bricklayers – a long and storied tradition of bricklayers who have encountered problems and found answers through the years.

Most pastors mistakenly believe, or act as though they believe, that a seminary degree equals qualification to lead and teach. Leadership is something that happens automatically, too many assume, by virtue of title or position. Ongoing training and practice is a luxury few have time to afford.

Yet, leadership, like brick-laying requires apprenticeship under a master craftsman. Growth requires discipline, practice and a community. To become and stay a skilled practitioner you must participate in the disciplines and practices of a community.

Growth comes through practice.

Chapter Seven Review:

In this chapter we looked at the fifth of seven tasks every leader must always do. Meet with your leadership team to complete and discuss the following exercise. Read each statement. Using the scale provided, indicate how true each statement is for your leadership team. Indicate how you really feel (not what you think you ought to.) Ask yourself: "Does this statement describe our actual habits and practices?"

If the statement is always true, place the number 5 on the line in front of the statement. If the statement is never true, then write the number 0 on the line. Place the number (0-5) that is the most accurate description of your actual leadership practice.

SCALE
5 = Always true.
4 = Often true.
3 = Sometimes true.
2 = Seldom true.
1 = Almost never true.
0 = Never true.

Please answer these statements referring to your actual practice. Be honest. Don't hesitate to choose a 5 or 0. Avoid using 3.

Feeding and nurturing the flock:
21) _____ When a need becomes known it is cared for immediately.
22) _____ Our preaching and teaching provides biblical "meat" for deep spiritual growth.
23) _____ We make intentional efforts to foster "one another community."
24) _____ We are growing through conversion: unbeliever professing faith in Jesus Christ.
25) _____ We are growing in discipleship: believers deepening their faith.

Compare and discuss your responses, asking questions such as:

"Why? What is it about us that we are thinking or acting this way?"

"What is God saying to us that we need to hear?"

"How long has this been true about us?" or "When did this start?"

"What would we need to do to address these results?"

Chapter Eight:
Mentoring and Equipping Leaders

When Jesus landed and saw a large crowd, he had compassion
on them, because they were like sheep without a shepherd.
So he began teaching them many things. Mark 6:34

Most protestant churches are organized around and dependent upon the personality and gifts of one person, the senior pastor. When this occurs, the church becomes a reflection of the leader. Where the leader is strong, the church is strong. Where the leader is weak, the church is weak. This is true of any leader and in any organization. No one person has the gifts, wisdom or strength to lead a people alone. All leaders have blind spots and weaknesses. Ignoring these truths forms the church in human, not divine image, and sets our leaders and churches up for failure.

The New Testament model for the church is never one person leading. The church is always pictured as a Body with many parts working together guided by leadership that functions as an interdependent team of complimentary gifted persons – apostles, prophets, evangelists, pastors and teachers. (Eph 4: 11-13)

Indeed, throughout Scripture, God calls, equips and appoints leadership teams of two or more people. "Though one may be overpowered," Solomon writes, " two can defend themselves. A cord of three strands is not quickly broken." (Eccl. 4:12.) Aaron teams with Moses; Jesus mobilizes twelve disciples and sends them out two by two, Paul teams up with Timothy and Silas while Barnabas travels with Mark.

The primary role of a leader, like a parent, is to "work him/herself out of a job" by equipping and mobilizing the saints to take on the ministry of the church. Spiritual leaders are always called to equip, never control. The primary difference between controlling and equipping is the subject or object of the action. Controlling is about self. Equipping is about others. To equip means to empower.

An effective leader will encourage the strengths and empower the gifts of others. At issue is how to be stewards of God's resources, not who gets the credit.

One test for measuring effectiveness is to imagine what would happen to the church if the leader was suddenly removed. If the church would fall immediately, then the leader, not gifted men and women that God has raised in the Body, is the focus of the church.

Every leader must equip the Body to be the church. As Paul says, the task of every leader is "to prepare God's people for works of service, so that the Body of Christ may be built up. (Eph 4: 12) The people are the ministers, not the leaders. Many pastors resist this because the pulpit is the one place where the pastor is safe, feels strong or speaks boldly. Out of the pulpit – in the home, the community or board room – the same person may be timid, weak or insecure, unable to take charge, make decisions or handle confrontation constructively.

Some pastors thrive in the pulpit but fail in the pew. They and their churches are formed around performance, not service.

Leaders who are facilitators, not performers

In a consumer driven culture the tendency of many churches is to be performance based. The church is established to meet needs and the leader is one who delivers or performs.

"If the leader meets my needs," each church member is taught to think, "then he/she is performing well." But, "when you stop meeting my needs, either the leader goes or I'm taking my family elsewhere."

In a performance based church the leader is performer. The leader can stay in the church as long as he or she knows, or appears to know, more than others.

Performance based leaders and churches set themselves up for failure. No one person knows everything or has all the answers. Afraid to admit this, the leader's only option is to be controlling and defensive. Pretending to know things, the leader is forced to hide sin and deny failure. The leader works alone. A church that is performance based forces leaders and followers into attitudes and actions that are contrary to Scripture.

The chart below illustrates the difference:

Attitude / Action	Performance-Based	Spirit-Led
Leader's role	Leader as performer	Leader as servant
Measured by	Success	Faithfulness
Leadership style	Controls: Rule-based	Facilitates: Obedience-based
Knowledge	Objective: Knows facts	Interpretive: Lives with uncertainty
Responsibility	Hides faults	Confesses sin
Ministry philosophy	Works alone	Builds a team
Image	"I am my position"	Discovering and growing in gifts

A story is told about the famous boxer Mohammed Ali flying across country with his equally famous ego. Before take-off the flight attendant went through the cabin to check seat belts. Noticing Ali was not wearing his she asked him to buckle up.

"Superman don't need no seat belt," Ali explained. "Superman don't need no plane," the attendant shot back.

There are no super heroes in the church. Leaders are called to serve, to discover, facilitate, learn, ask questions, and live by faith with uncertainty. Faith is not the substance of what we know and can prove but what we don't know and cannot prove, yet believe.

One of the first churches we served suffered from what we called "a cancer of autonomy." The church was dying because of a cycle of conflict over many years. People were gossiping about leaders and ministries were fighting one another. They were not practicing biblical community. Instead everyone retreated to their comfort zones for cover.

"If we have a cancer," we said, "then we have to take radical steps to cut it out."

We recommended that the church close for two months. In place of all existing ministries and programs, some of which were healthy, we would gather for worship, Bible study and Body life as a community. We would learn how to love, submit and serve one another.

This meant that the youth would not go on their retreat, the Bible study for our over 60 seniors would not meet and the women's ministry would be postponed. The evangelism teams would not go out. People would not be saved. When some questioned canceling evangelism we pointed out that sin has a high cost. "The Jesus we proclaim is not the Jesus we are living and the Jesus we are living is not a god worth believing in," we said to the church. This got their attention.

The women in the church had an active ministry with 150 women who had paid dues to come for Bible study and crafts each week. Now I was proposing that they weren't going to meet. I asked to meet with the leaders of the group, many of whom no longer attended the church.

"Here is what I believe we are to do," I said. I was sitting in a room, the only man with twelve women, describing the plan with its implications. The look on their faces indicated that the idea was not being received well.

"How do you know this idea is going to work?" one woman asked.

"I don't know it's going to work," I said.

"When you have done this before, what happened?" another asked.

"I've never done this before," I replied.

"Then how do you know this is God's will?" a third woman asked.

"I don't know." I said. "I believe it is. What I am asking you to do is pray about it this week and sincerely ask God if this is something we should do." "Will you do that?" I asked.

They agreed. By the end of the week, I had received ten phone calls and letters from the women. Most said something like this, "Jim I hate the idea. I don't think it is going to work and I think it will destroy this church . . . but I think God wants us to do it." So, we did. In the next six months God helped us all learn and practice biblical community.

The point of this story is not to recommend the method but the process. Leaders must be able to say, "I don't know. I believe. Will you walk with me in faith trusting God to show us His will?" Leadership is an invitation to faith in God, not in the leader.

A servant leader is willing to follow the Lord and take risks. If God intervenes, the glory is His. If our understanding was flawed or the ideas fail, the leader can humbly take responsibility. No one was under any illusion that the pastor "had a special word from God," or was leading by his own strength.

When pastors are forced or decide to be performers, they often find themselves taking credit for their success and blaming others for their failure because they have to keep up a persona in order to keep their job.

Preparing people for service

Leaders "prepare God's people for works of service." This means identifying, equipping, and mentoring gifted people to minister together interdependently – empowering and equipping others to discover, use, and grow in their gifts to glorify God and to edify the Body.

Observing leadership in most churches, Paul's description of leadership in Ephesians chapter four may be one of the most ignored or misunderstood in Scripture. Several points should be noted briefly.

First, Paul pictures team, not individual, leadership. Apostles, prophets, evangelists, pastors and teachers work together to prepare God's people. Church leadership is never a one man show.

Second, it is the people, not the leaders, who do the works of service. The role of the apostles, prophets, evangelists, pastors and teachers is preparation. The people are the ministers. The Body does the work of ministry, not the leaders.

Third, the church builds up in unity and grows up in maturity in direct proportion to the teamwork of leaders and involvement of members – each part doing its work. In other words, it is not the pastor, but the "whole" body joined together, that grows and builds.

Note how here, again, the emphasis is on maturing out of infancy. Paul is saying that a church whose leaders do not equip members to grow and build themselves will be a church unable to discern truth from error.

This is why the apostles decided that the primary function of spiritual leadership in the church is to "give attention to prayer and the ministry of the word." As the church after Pentecost blossomed and spread, practical leadership issues emerged: "In those days when the number of disciples was increasing, the Grecian Jews among them complained against the Hebraic Jews because their widows were being overlooked in the daily distribution of food. So the Twelve gathered all the disciples together and said, "It would not be right for us to neglect the ministry of the word of God in order to wait on tables. Brothers, choose seven men from among you who are known to be full of the Spirit and wisdom. We will turn this responsibility over to them and will give our attention to prayer and the ministry of the word." (Acts 6: 1-7)

The apostles recognized the limits of their calling. They recognized that others were better able and suited to serve. So they empowered the church to recognize and to employ the gifts God had provided. Deacons were people recognized by the Body as men "full of the Spirit and wisdom." They were given responsibility and freedom to act within their gifting.

Preparing people means equipping all members to discover, utilize and grow in their "gifts of grace" – their spiritual gifts. It means putting the right people in the right places. "Rightness" is measured by identifying and affirming grace.

Shirley was the name of my first ewe. Shirley was friendly and easy to approach, the ideal ewe for a flock. Being first to the shepherd, the other sheep took their cues from Shirley. Shirley became my "lead sheep."

In ancient shepherding, just like today, every flock had "lead sheep." These sheep were usually the older ewes who knew the shepherd's voice and trusted the shepherd's care and protection. The lead sheep were the first to follow. As the lead sheep trusted and followed the shepherd, so the flock trusted and followed the lead sheep.

Our two pastures are divided by a dirt road with several flower and vegetable gardens alongside. A constant fear in our home each summer is of the sheep getting out of the pasture and into the flowers and herbs and vegetables. Every so often the sheep do get out. When someone spots them he calls to the others, "the sheep are out!" Our family snaps into action like the local volunteer rescue squad. The routine was simple: get Shirley's attention and lead her back to the pasture (usually with a cup of grain.) Shirley follows the shepherd, and the other sheep follow Shirley. Simple.

But our summers are also spent entertaining many guests, friends who do not know Shirley nor our routine. In their desire to help when the sheep got out, they would do the very worst thing. They chased the sheep or tried to herd the sheep like cows. The sheep would scatter in every direction and into every garden. A small nuisance suddenly became a huge problem.

The greatest fear of any shepherd is a divided flock.

Leading the flock means keeping the flock together. A divided flock is impossible to lead. Keeping the flock together requires both skill and loyalty.

But biblical shepherding must never be a process of coercion. A shepherd does not push or badger. Leadership draws people in, rather than push them on. It is going out in front, having the trust of those behind. The good shepherd will know all his sheep, but will also select a few sheep to know well whom he can trust to help lead.

Recently, we started a new flock of sheep on our farm. We had been away from our farm for two years and had sold off our other flock. Now we were starting new with six yearlings purchased from two different sheep farms. All of the sheep were young, new to each other and new to us. This meant that there were no lead sheep and no recognition of my voice as shepherd. Simply put, there was no relationship.

When I entered my pasture the first few times, the sheep were skittish running off in one direction, then another. They always ran together. Sheep know that personal safety is in staying close to the flock. (Similarly, when sheep wander they usually wander together.) Twice a day for several weeks I took grain into the pasture, spread it out and sat down a safe distance away. The sheep came to eat keeping wary eyes on me. If I moved suddenly to swat a fly or sneeze, the sheep would bolt. So I sat still for several minutes speaking softly to the animals so they could get to know my voice.

Each day I sat a little closer to the grain and spoke louder to the sheep, assigning names to each. After weeks of observing and being with the sheep a relationship of trust was built. I knew which sheep were emerging as dominant and which would follow. Shepherding takes trust and trust is earned over time – by listening and being present with the sheep.

Today in the West, any Christian can find more spiritual food than he or she could possibly consume. Christian books, tapes, media and the internet are readily available and packaged in ways most local church pastors cannot match. But consuming spiritual food does not equal spiritual growth, nor is this the church. God's design is for people to grow in relationship – to Himself and to one another. This is impossible outside of the church. Biblical leadership requires relationship.

Sheep always graze together. In fact, an animal that feeds alone is usually a sign of sickness. So it is in the church. The church is not the sum of information consumed or knowledge attained. It is the people of God – living, loving, learning and lifting the Name of Jesus Christ together.

The church is a called together people. There is no church outside of a gathered community – people interacting personally with one another in submission to Christ. There is no virtual church. There are no "lone ranger" Christians.

We are made for each other. Shepherd leaders are called to listen, learn and live with the flock. It may not be possible for a shepherd to know every member of the flock well, but every shepherd must be available to and trusted by the sheep. A leader who does not enter into the life of his congregation is not a shepherd.

Jesus spent time with people. He listened, asked questions and told stories. He was known by many. Yet Jesus chose twelve disciples who would spread the Gospel to all nations. Further, He selected Peter, James and John as "lead sheep." Similarly, a leader must build a team of trusted leaders to help lead the church.

The effective leader will cultivate "lead sheep," a few elders and lay people who share a deeper intimacy and understanding of the pastor than others. There is obvious danger in this, of course, and it should never alienate the flock or become a group unto itself. Motives and sensitivities must be checked. But the presence of a smaller group of intimates will benefit the pastor as well as flock, as it did Jesus and His disciples – because the process will raise up, affirm and build new leaders. A leader disciples people to make new leaders.

Chapter Eight Review:

In this chapter we looked at the sixth of seven tasks every leader must always do. Meet with your leadership team to complete and discuss the following exercise. Read each statement. Using the scale provided, indicate how true each statement is for your leadership team. Indicate how you really feel (not what you think you ought to.) Ask yourself: "Does this statement describe our actual habits and practices?"

If the statement is always true, place the number 5 on the line in front of the statement. If the statement is never true, then write the number 0 on the line. Place the number (0-5) that is the most accurate description of your actual leadership practice.

SCALE
5 = Always true.
4 = Often true.
3 = Sometimes true.
2 = Seldom true.
1 = Almost never true.
0 = Never true.

Please answer these statements referring to your actual practice. Be honest. Don't hesitate to choose a 5 or 0. Avoid using 3.

Mentoring and equipping leaders:

26) _____ We have an intentional, coordinated and effective process to identify, recruit and mentor future leaders.

27) _____ All present leaders are in a spiritual accountability group.

28) _____ We provide ongoing, effective training for present leaders.

29) _____ We are implementing an effective process for equipping members to discover, grow in and use spiritual gifts.

30) _____ We work together as an interdependent team – based upon affirmed gifts and skills.

Compare and discuss your responses, asking questions such as:

"Why? What is it about us that we are thinking or acting this way?"

"What is God saying to us that we need to hear?"

"How long has this been true about us?" or "When did this start?"

"What would we need to do to address these results?"

Chapter Nine:
Modeling and Forming Character

*Be shepherds of God's flock that is under your care, serving
as overseers – not because you must, but because you are willing,
as God wants you to be; not greedy for money,
but eager to serve. 1Pet. 5:2*

In our work with fallen leaders and troubled churches we have
discovered three critical factors that determine the long-term health of a
ministry leader: 1.) his or her character; 2.) the character of his or her
spouse, and 3.) his or her regular involvement in life-on-life accountability. (The absence or weakness in one or more of these three key
factors will inevitably result in a leader sabotaging, and often hurting
deeply, his or her marriage, family, and ministry.)

Scripture continually emphasizes character before competency. Yet
most churches focus on competency before character when selecting
leaders. This is why many churches fail or become stagnant. No church
can rise above the character of its leaders.

God calls the church to "be holy and blameless" (Eph 1:4), to
"change our mind" in and through the church.

Leaders live out the character traits of Scripture, while calling others
to transformation. While we might consider dozens of biblical virtues the
following four are essential for every leader and every church: brokenness, courage, integrity and justice. Each represents the Lordship of
Christ over an area of life. Brokenness is Lordship in Heart. Courage is
Lordship in action. Integrity is Lordship in common life, or community.
Justice is Lordship in society. As we will see, all four are necessary to
keep the leader and church in proper balance.

Brokenness

Brokenness is contrition, a kind of faith in the heart. Without
brokenness we cannot come to Christ. Without brokenness we cannot
lead.

Brokenness is common to all biblical leaders. Abraham, Sarah, Moses, Joseph, Rehab, Hannah, Samuel, David, Esther, Isaiah, Jeremiah, Mary, Jesus, Peter, Paul, and others all were broken either through sin, failure, hardship, testing, discipline, or suffering.

Brokenness is a distinctly Christian notion that allows, in fact insists upon, weakness being strength. "My grace is sufficient for you, for my power is made perfect in weakness.' Therefore I will boast all the more gladly about my weaknesses, so that Christ's power may rest on me. That is why, for Christ's sake, I delight in weaknesses, in insults, in hardships, in persecutions, in difficulties. For when I am weak, then I am strong." (2Cor. 12:9-10).

Brokenness understands that grace is unmerited favor and, while free, is never cheap or easy.

We have been disturbed to find that most churches do not practice confession and forgiveness or, if they do, do so with what Dietrich Bonhoeffer called "cheap grace" – minimizing the responsibility and consequences of sin by trying to make the problem go away. Forgiveness is the beginning of a redemptive process, not the end. The key to transformation is making restitution and reconstituting the habits of thinking and behaving that led to the problem in the first place. Biblical restoration requires learning through brokenness that goes well beyond forgiveness.

Brokenness is the constant awareness, attitude, and life practice that all a leader is, and does, is nothing apart from God's grace. It is the emptying of oneself fully to God's reign and purpose in one's life. All great biblical leaders were broken. Perhaps this is why so many of the leaders in Scripture were shepherds of sheep first. Remember Moses? When he saw an Egyptian mistreating an Israelite, he intervened in his own strength, killing the Egyptian. But when he tried to stop two Israelites from quarreling, he was rebuked. So Moses fled, to spend forty years as a shepherd, learning that leadership is not by strength of will but trust in God. Shepherding is hard, lonely and backbreaking work that God used often to break the will of those who would lead His flock. Scripture tells of leaders who are broken in various ways – from sin, failure, hardship, testing, discipline or suffering. Yet, brokenness cannot be earned. It is a gift from God.

Courage

If brokenness is the first character trait of a spiritual leader, courage must be the second.

Two years ago we served a church that was in the midst of a leadership crisis brought on by the sin and subsequent cover-up of a leader in the church. Our recommendation to the church was that the senior pastor, three associate staff, and the entire elder board resign. As you might imagine, this seemed harsh and drastic to many in the church, but after prayer and reflection they decided to accept the recommendation and trust God for healing. We helped the church find an interim pastor who led the church through reconciliation to unity and growth. The church had to trust God through many hardships and uncertainties but the leaders and members were faithful and the church is much healthier as a result of the experience. A new senior pastor now leads this vital church.

A broken person will admit failure and confess sin. A courageous person will do it in the midst of risk and uncertainty.

Brokenness and courage must be the combined character traits of every spiritual leader. Brokenness without courage results in weak fatalism – a man or woman who plays the victim. Courage without brokenness is arrogance – a man or woman that trusts in methods or human performance.

Richard Bush, a Christian leader and member of our board, recently reminded me that most movements of God in Scripture were preceded by the call to "be strong and courageous" in His strength. (See Deut. 31:6-7,23; Josh. 1:6-7,9,18;1Chr. 28:20; 2Chr.15:8; 2Chr. 32:7; Matt. 14:27;.Acts 4:13; Acts 23:11; Acts 27:22,25; 1Cor. 16:13;. Phil.1:14,20; Heb. 3:6)

The Christmas narrative is all about brokenness and courage. In the Gospel of Luke the angel Gabriel announces the birth of John the Baptist and the birth of Jesus with the same words, "do not be afraid." Mary responds in faith. "I am the Lord's servant (brokenness). May it be to me as you have said" (courage).

Courage marks the opposing balance to brokenness. Courage is the shepherd protecting the flock from any danger or threat. Courage is a constant awareness, attitude, and life practice that a leader can do all things through Christ's strength. Courage is a boldness of heart and mind which enables a leader to encounter danger and difficulty with confidence and conviction. It is taking faith-filled risk grounded in a hope and a trust that God is greater than obstacles or circumstances. Courage always involves risk because it requires taking action before, and often in the absence of, any guarantee or proof of a positive outcome.

Christian courage is locating ones thought, action, and outcome in God's promises. Yet courage without brokenness is arrogance. True courage places trust in God, not in oneself.

Integrity

As the focus of brokenness and courage tends to be on the leader, integrity and justice will look at our relationship with others. First we look inward. Integrity is oneness, a collective commitment to "one Lord, one faith, one baptism; one God and Father of all, who is over all and through all and in all." It is a leader and community becoming "of one mind," or "of one accord. The English word for "integrity" comes from the word "integer" referring to a "whole number," a "complete entity," or something "undivided." In biblical terms, integrity is being undivided in our relationship with God and others.

Marriage and family are frequent metaphors for the church in Scripture. As husband and wife become one, so the church is called to oneness. As children reflect the character of mother and father, so the church is formed by the character of leaders. Shepherding is spiritual parenting – involving the same instincts, attributes and sensitivities of a godly mother and father. A shepherd is a life-giving parent.

For Paul, this is not about nurture alone. He links leadership to marriage and effective parenting. This is virtue and skill. Leaders will show integrity in the church as they practice fidelity in their marriage. Leaders are "parents" to the flock, just as they are parents in the home.

The church should consider the qualifications of leaders for these character traits because leadership, like marriage and parenting, is character forming. The way a leader leads will form those who follow. The assumption is that home and church are indelibly linked. In fact, Paul describes the church as an extended family, a "household." He exhorts husbands and wives to respect and love one another because their marriage is a picture of Christ's relationship to the church.

All of these are "one" – leader, family and church.

Integrity is at the very heart of leadership. "Oneness" is everything for the church and must be foremost for a shepherd especially in crisis or failure. Yet it is here – when confronted with our failures – that so many leaders and churches stumble, opting for the values of our narcissistic and individualistic culture against a way of life shaped by the cross practiced in one another community. Failure is a crucible of character.

We recently served a church that had seen its congregation decline 40% in ten years, due in great part to the failure of the senior pastor to lead and shepherd the flock.

The senior pastor refused to own his failure. Instead, he repeatedly used the following responses to shift responsibility for his actions:

1. Blame: The pastor constantly stated that a major problem in the church was the congregation's "lack of commitment," going so far as to telling the church, "you have made me what I have become." This pastor actually told his congregation that, "I'd be a better shepherd if you were better sheep." He had the shepherd following the sheep, rather than the shepherd calling, nurturing and growing the flock.

2. Hurt: A constant claim of the pastor was that people have "hurt" him, failing to distinguish how hurt can be both productive and redemptive. (Proverbs 27:5-6)

3. Position: The pastor insisted that "God called him" to the church and that "I will not leave until God tells me to."

These statements had some measure of truth. Some people did lack commitment. Some did treat the pastor unkindly. We did not question the pastor's original call.

What was troublesome was the pastor's use of these responses to divert and to excuse his own responsibility.

A good question to ask in these situations is "who is the object and subject of this concern or statement?"

Every instance above has the same object and subject: the pastor. Responsibility, feelings and power were all about and for the benefit of the shepherd, not the sheep.

In other words, the pastor was not "one" with his congregation. Integrity was broken.

Integrity is broken whenever a leader's needs become primary, over (or against) the Lordship of Jesus Christ and the needs of others. This is the root of all leadership failure.

When this happens the church cannot practice or embody redemption. Instead of a leader sharing his heart, owning his fault and taking biblical steps to restore patterns of failure, a privatized faith and bankrupt grace is proclaimed. This is not biblical Christianity, nor leadership.

When the church is truly the church, leaders and members alike are committed to transform and grow as one – in submission to the Lordship of Jesus Christ. Here, we are not surprised by sin nor failure, nor condemned to work out our salvation in secrecy or alone. Rather, the motivation is to rush into the light of others so that we might confess, receive forgiveness and work out restitution and restoration.

This rarely happens in the church because we lack integrity. We cling instead to our rights and reputations, unaware that our lives, despite our words, are forming harassed and helpless sheep.

Here, again, we see how the image of a flock gives greater insight and understanding. Sheep, by natural instinct, know that their safety is in staying together. A flock is a picture of oneness. Understood in this light, integrity is far more than honesty. It is the constant interest in, and action taken, based upon the needs of others. But inward looking can also become unbalanced. That is why the leader and church must also exhibit justice.

Justice

The ancient shepherd had to beware of many threats to the flock. Between mountain lions and bears, hyenas and jackals, predators were a constant threat. Every Near Eastern shepherd carried a rod and a sling for protection.

The rod was a thick club about 18 inches long. Sometimes iron nails were driven into the end, making it a more effective weapon. The rod was used to defend both sheep and shepherd alike. Rescuing a sheep often meant risking your life.

The sling was made of leather, gathered in a pouch connected by two long strands of leather about 24 inches long. During idle time a shepherd practiced slinging stones. Putting a stone in the pouch and whirling the sling overhead, a practiced shepherd could drop a stone or hit a target with tremendous force and amazing accuracy.

In the twenty-third Psalm, David says he won't fear even when facing death because the Shepherd is with him; "your rod and your staff, they comfort me."

The protection of the shepherd is a comfort to the sheep. The rod is a defensive weapon. The staff is not a weapon at all, but a walking stick. The staff was a stout pole about six to eight feet long that kept a shepherd from falling when walking on rough terrain or fording a river. So comfort comes from leading and protecting. The Apostle Peter, in the same letter he instructs elders to "shepherd the flock of God," warns just four verse later to, "Be self-controlled and alert. Your enemy the devil prowls around like a roaring lion looking for someone to devour." (1Pet. 5:8)

Several years ago a messianic Jewish Rabbi told me about the daily custom of Torah readings in the Temple. From the time the law was first given to the Israelites and a temple was built, verses from the Torah were read daily. In fact, a record is kept of what was read for every day of the year during the last three thousand years.

To the Hebrew mind, every event has purpose. There are no mistakes. God is sovereign and works all things to His good purpose. That is why Hebrew tradition relates special events to daily readings.

With this understanding, the story that unfolds in Luke chapter four is especially profound. Jesus has just returned to Galilee from the wilderness, being tempted by Satan for forty days. Entering Nazareth on the Sabbath, he went to the synagogue as was his custom. At the point in the service where the Torah portion is read, Jesus is asked to read. He stands, opens the scroll to the daily reading and declares, "The Spirit of the Lord is on me, because he has anointed me to preach good news to the poor. He has sent me to proclaim freedom for the prisoners and recovery of sight for the blind, to release the oppressed, to proclaim the year of the Lord's favor." (Luke 4:18-19)

Jesus rolled up the scroll, gave it back to the attendant and sat down. Then Jesus began to teach beginning with the remarkable statement, "Today this scripture is fulfilled in your hearing."

Jesus summarizes his ministry with this quote from Isaiah 61, a chapter that proclaims God's justice. Note the people Jesus comes to serve: the poor, the brokenhearted, the captive, prisoners, and those who mourn. (Isaiah 61: 1-3)

The call to justice is repeated throughout Old and New Testaments as the people of God are to have continual regard for those who are hungry, for widows, strangers, aliens, and the weak.

Hospitality, for example is a moral imperative. The word hospitality literally means showing love to strangers. God's people are to be like the good Samaritan, people who welcome strangers and treat them justly. For the Israelites, being compassionate and just to strangers was a way of remembering their own exile and wandering. For believers today, hospitality provides a sacred space where we practice the virtues of giving and receiving. Leaders, it follows, ought to be those who open their homes to those in need.

When the apostle Paul was given the right hand of fellowship and commissioned to preach the gospel to the Gentiles, the only requirement placed upon him was that he "should continue to remember the poor," the very thing Paul says he was eager to do. (Gal. 2:10)

Justice is missing in many churches because few leaders are "eager" to remember the poor. In most churches, justice is either ignored completely, or it becomes a pre-occupation leading to self-righteousness. But if the Gospel is to be lived out as well as proclaimed, the church will be known by its love in community and justice in society. This means far more than a voice, it means action.

The shepherd leader will know and seek to actively address the issues of justice in the region the church resides. For some this may mean feeding the hungry in soup kitchens, coming alongside teenage girls in pregnancy crisis centers, or offering loving counsel and support to homo-sexuals with AIDS. For others it will mean leading bible studies in prisons, offering recovery for the addicted or providing child care for single parents.

The godly leader and effective church will be known for acts of justice, offered as unto the Lord.

"For I was hungry and you gave me nothing to eat, I was thirsty and you gave me nothing to drink, I was a stranger and you did not invite me in, I needed clothes and you did not clothe me, I was sick and in prison and you did not look after me.' "They also will answer, ëLord, when did we see you hungry or thirsty or a stranger or needing clothes or sick or in prison, and did not help you?' "He will reply, ëI tell you the truth, whatever you did not do for one of the least of these, you did not do for me.' " Matt. 25:42-45

Shepherding is all about defending the weak from the attacks of the strong. A shepherd must practice justice.

Justice is the outward work of mercy, compassion and moral right-ness within and beyond the flock. In the Christian leader, justice is the quality of heart and action to serve and honor the well-being of the poor, weak and disenfranchised. Justice embodies the mission and ministry of Jesus. Justice is faith looking outward. Justice is how the church becomes and displays a community of righteousness. The way a leader and church respond to and address issues like violence, racism and hatred will prove the power of the Gospel. Justice is the crucible of authentic community.

Summary

The godly leader will model and help form each of these virtues in balance. Balance is vital. Brokenness without Courage produces victims and skepticism. Courage without Brokenness produces arrogance and mere human performance. Integrity (oneness) without Justice produces cliques, even cults. Justice without Integrity produces self-righteousness. Each in proportion to the other can produce a living community of Christ.

Chapter Nine Review:

In this chapter we looked at the last of seven tasks every leader must always do. Meet with your leadership team to complete and discuss the following exercise. Read each statement. Using the scale provided, indicate how true each statement is for your leadership team. Indicate how you really feel (not what you think you ought to.) Ask yourself: "Does this statement describe our actual habits and practices?"

If the statement is always true, place the number 5 on the line in front of the statement. If the statement is never true, then write the number 0 on the line. Place the number (0-5) that is the most accurate description of your actual leadership practice.

SCALE
5 = Always true.
4 = Often true.
3 = Sometimes true.
2 = Seldom true.
1 = Almost never true.
0 = Never true.

Please answer these statements referring to your actual practice. Be honest. Don't hesitate to choose a 5 or 0. Avoid using 3.

Modeling and forming character:
31) _____ We live out the character traits for spiritual leaders in Scripture.
32) _____ We model brokenness: humility – constant awareness that we can do nothing apart from Christ.
33) _____ We model courage: boldness – constant awareness that we can do all things in Christ's strength.
34) _____ We model integrity: oneness – unity – being undivided in our relationship with God and others.
35) _____ We model justice: mercy – intent upon serving and honoring the well-being of the poor and weak.

Compare and discuss your responses, asking questions such as:

"Why? What is it about us that we are thinking or acting this way?"

"What is God saying to us that we need to hear?"

"How long has this been true about us?" or "When did this start?"

"What would we need to do to address these results?"

Section Review

In this section we looked at the seven tasks of a spiritual leader. At the end of each chapter you were asked to meet with your leadership team to grade leadership performance in each of the seven areas. Turn back to those chapter reviews and discuss the questions below:

Write, in the space below, the top strengths and weaknesses of your leadership team.

In the space below, make notes then discuss why and how your leadership team may be missing the mark:

Spend time in prayer asking God to give you wisdom – ears to hear, and eyes to see – how He may be calling you/your leadership team to change. Allow moments of silence.

After a season of prayer, discuss what you believe God is revealing. Agree upon three steps that you can take in the days ahead to respond to God's leading.

SECTION THREE:
Why We Must Recover Why

For the Lamb at the center of the throne will be their shepherd;
he will lead them to springs of living water. And God will wipe
away every tear from their eyes. Revelation 7:17

There is an old saying that goes something like this: "Those who merely know how or what, will always work for those who know why." Leadership is about why. Management is about how and what. What the church (and all organizations) needs most is leaders, not managers.

Jesus was a leader, not a manager. In fact, the Gospels record only two subjects where Jesus gave specific how-to or what-to-do steps to his disciples: how to pray (Luke 11:2) and how to be reconciled (Mat 18: 15-20). In most matters Jesus called people to a faith that required hearing, interpreting and taking steps to obey in absence of specific instructions.

Jesus gave the why and allowed His followers to figure out how. He gave pictures, questions or instructions designed to be obeyed, not copied.

Leadership, for Jesus, was an invitation into a way of life, not a set of laws or methods to be followed. Yet, this stands in contrast to the formulaic teaching and writing on leadership common today. Go to any bookstore (particularly a Christian bookstore) and you will find enumerable titles that begin with the word "how."

To lead like Jesus we must reclaim spiritual discovery over human method; restoring the "why" over our preoccupation with "how-to." This is a theological issue as well as a practical one, and it starts with fundamental notions of what the church is for.

In previous sections we have explored how the role and purpose of ancient shepherding can give us clues to leadership in the church. But why the church? The apostle Paul tells us we were chosen before the creation of the world to be holy and blameless (Eph. 1:4). God's intent, Paul says, "was that now, through the church, the manifold wisdom of God should be made known to the rulers and authorities in the heavenly realms, according to his eternal purpose which he accomplished in Christ

Jesus our Lord" (Eph 3:10).

Note: Scripture is describing the "what" and "why" of the church, not the "how." "Being" always precedes "doing." The church embodies and declares God's purpose in Christ. In Christ, the church lives as a present earthly gathering of a coming, heavenly Kingdom. The subject is always God; never us or our good ideas.

This means that our salvation, hope and very existence have purposes far beyond our needs and goals. God calls us to be formed by eternal values that both precede and follow us. Scripture welcomes us into a narrative that was founded before time and is leading inexorably to a certain end. Believers are sojourners made for a coming world who locate themselves in the church as a visible, spiritual representation of what is yet to come.

To be the Church is to declare Christ's Lordship over our time, family, marriage, ministry and all of life.

Is your church formed around methodology or theology? Is your church more like a business or a body? How-to churches tend to make personal needs, not holiness, their why – their reason for being. This produces fruit that looks like autonomy rather than diversity, prosperity (feel good now) not the cross (suffering and self-surrender) and a spirituality that is Self-conscious instead of Christ-revealing.

In contrast, the Kingdom of Christ suggests a fundamental solution: holiness founded in the cross, self-surrender and obedient response to a glorified Christ. The Church must return to a theology of the cross. We must change the way we think and act, turning from self-directed methodologies to habits and practices of a holy and separate people.

This will happen as leaders become spiritual shepherds.

In the two short chapters that follow we will look briefly at the three callings the church is to fulfill and the one word that summarizes spiritual leadership.

Chapter Ten:
Why the Church

*For you were like sheep going astray, but now you have returned
to the Shepherd and Overseer of your souls. 1Pet. 2:25*

In Acts chapter two, Luke paints three defining characteristics of the church, three callings we are to fulfill: (1) a living Body, (2) a learning community, and (3) a loving fellowship.

A living Body

Godly life requires the church. We go to church to live.

All of Scripture speaks to the people of God as a living hope and the Church as a living system, a Holy priesthood, a Bride, a Body.

By understanding the Church as a living process, rather than an institution, believers are free to make commitments and face hardship based upon a future hope and the present, active indwelling presence of God in our midst. In other words, God turns the values, power and wisdom of this world upside down through the foolishness and weakness of the cross. In Christ, and Christ alone, the Church is made alive.

Like all living things, growth in the church requires change, death and renewal. Pain, suffering and even death may be embraced in faith under a sovereign, redemptive purpose. Our nature wants to control, predict and keep stable. God urges us to trust, to obey, to die and grow.

The church is a vital living organism: not a keeper of knowledge or method, but rather the teller of a story. It is not a need-meeting machine, but a living, forgiving system. People are not simple automatons, nor are they bundles of self-esteem. Scripture is not a therapy or an owner's manual. The church is not about our needs.

Instead, the Church is a historical and complex living reality that is dynamically interconnected and regenerating. The church cannot be controlled or engineered.

A learning community

Second, the Church is a learning community that hears, responds and embodies God's salvation-story. That is, the church grows by living and speaking the Gospel story. Out of the story of faith the church is formed and learns – how to love God with all our heart and soul and mind and strength, and how to love our neighbor as we love ourselves. It learns all of this through Jesus.

George MacDonald once wrote, "It is the man Jesus we have to know, and the Bible we use to that end – not for theory or dogma."

The Church – the Body of Christ – renews itself by drawing life from its Creator through the power of the Holy Spirit. That is why Paul speaks of spiritual gifts given to grow the Body. The Body grows as it learns together – hands and feet and eyes and ears. Learning always requires others.

In fact, we cannot know or learn about God apart from the life of the Body. No truth can be known fully by one person. Rather, the Body needs each member to hear, test and discern God's voice. Christian learning is necessarily communal. In fact, Paul tells the Ephesians that their spiritual growth is directly related to their ability to speak truth into one another's lives in love (Eph 4:15).

Here, we begin to understand that learning is not, fundamentally, about the mind, but about hearing and obeying, often without understanding. Faith comes by hearing, not sight. It is in doing God's will that we understand His good purpose. God gives us His word, His Spirit and His people to hear and discern His voice. Scripture is written to and for a people, not individuals and should be received in kind, read out loud often so that it might be heard.

Jesus' prayer was for the Spirit to guide believers into truth, even clean them by it, so that we may be one.

A loving fellowship

Finally, the Church is a loving fellowship. Jesus, the fulfillment of the Old Testament Promise, is love incarnate. Paul exhorts the Philippian church to have the mind of Christ, to lead a life of sacrificial love. Paul tells the Corinthians that everything is loss without love. The apostle John calls the Church to love God and to love each other. Love is of God. Any who profess to believe in God but do not love their brothers, do not know God.

Love is the basis of our relationship to God and with one another. It is the motivation for and the result of both worship and evangelism.

"A new command I give you," Jesus tells His disciples, "to love one another." The church must be a community characterized not by uniformity – loving those who love you or agree with you – but by unified diversity, loving and fellowshipping with those who you would otherwise never be drawn to apart from Christ.

Jesus turns human love from self to sacrifice. The cross calls the church to follow His example. Such love draws women and men to the Savior.

The Church is a living picture of this loving relationship. The symbol that helps us participate most in telling and re-telling the story of Jesus is the Eucharist. In the Eucharist, the Church celebrates the greatest example of love: Christ's atoning death on the cross. Communion is a time of holiness when we personally and corporately acknowledge the sovereignty of God and proclaim Christ's resurrection. In humility we confess our sin, make ourselves right with one another and make ourselves ready for the Groom. At the name of Jesus, every knee bows. The Church declares Jesus, Lord and Savior over all.

What kind of leader?

If this is the "why" of church, what kind of leader will best recover and model God's calling to the church? Here again, Scripture speaks of "why" far more than "how." In fact, biblical leadership always values character above skill.

For a living Body: a leader who listens

If the church is a living Body then the leader must listen to the One who gives life. The word vocation is founded in hearing and responding to a "voice." All leadership starts with listening: all Christian leadership begins with hearing and responding to God's call. Audition precedes vision. Martin Luther once said, "to see God we must place our eyes in our ears." The primary function of a leader is to hear and interpret God's voice through His Word, by His Spirit and through His people.

For a learning community: a leader who follows

If the church is a learning community then the leader must be an authentic follower of Christ – one who faithfully puts into words and practice what God is saying. This is more than teaching or preaching; it is embodying the habits and practices of following Jesus. The task of the leader is to lead people on a path of discovery – to learn by listening, reflecting, hearing and obeying God's voice. The leader is to continually and truthfully evaluate where the church is in light of God's vision and, by living the vision, encourage and exhort the Body to grow as well.

For a loving fellowship: a leader who invites

If the church is a loving community then the leader must be one who invites the people of God into loving relationship with Christ and with each other. We invite people to consider the truth claims of Christ; to explore as well as experience what it would look like to be formed by the life, death and resurrection of Jesus Christ. We invite people into a story that remembers God's faithfulness through thousands of years. We invite people to a table where the bread and the cup look back to Christ's sacrifice while looking forward to the marriage supper of the lamb.

Leaders hear, obey and invite others to a way of life shaped by the cross.

Chapter Eleven:
Why Leadership

When they had finished eating, Jesus said to Simon Peter, "Simon son of John, do you truly love me more than these?" "Yes, Lord," he said, "you know that I love you." Jesus said, "Feed my lambs." Again Jesus said, "Simon son of John, do you truly love me?" He answered, "Yes, Lord, you know that I love you." Jesus said, "Take care of my sheep." The third time he said to him, "Simon son of John, do you love me?" Peter was hurt because Jesus asked him the third time, "Do you love me?" He said, "Lord, you know all things; you know that I love you." Jesus said, "Feed my sheep. John 21: 15-17

One summer evening several years ago when I went out to the barn to feed the sheep, I noticed a lamb was missing.

Re-counting each animal, I again came up one short. I went looking for the missing lamb.

I looked for about ten minutes without any sign. Then I called and listened. A faint bleating sound came back. It was the lamb on the other side of the pasture lying on its side. When I got over to the lamb I saw it's leg was caught in wire. It had been struggling for hours. The lamb was weak and breathing hard.

When I untangled the wire, the lamb tried to get up and walk but fell back down, exhausted. I had to carry it back to the barn.

If you have ever tried to carry a lamb you know it is something like carrying a sack of potatoes. The best way to carry a lamb is on your shoulders, legs strapped around each side of your head.

I remember thinking as I was walking back to the barn, my lost lamb straddled upon my shoulders, about the parable of the lost sheep. A warm feeling came over me as I imagined myself a "good shepherd."

But as I walked, suddenly I had another warm feeling – a wet, warm feeling that went down my neck and under my shirt and ran all the way down my back.

Many leaders have a romantic view of shepherding. But shepherding is hard and dirty work. Being a shepherd of the flock of God will require the spiritual equivalent of "mucking out the barn." It means being with the sheep when the sheep are hurting and dirty and are more likely to use you, than appreciate your ministry.

When I was an assistant pastor after graduating from college, Sharon and I lived in a small house on the property where our new church building was being built. The house was small but sturdy. We thought it was great. It had its problems though, not the least of which was an old and broken septic system.

One day, after struggling with a septic problem, I called a septic service to come pump out our tank. The truck pulled up and out jumped a young man my age at the time – about 23. As he took the lid off the system and readied the hose to pump, we struck up a conversation standing over the open sewer.

He asked if I owned the house. I said, "No, the church owns it."

"You work in the church?" he asked both puzzled and amazed.

"Yes. I'm an assistant pastor."

"A pastor, huh?" he replied.

Then he said something I'll never forget. "I can't understand why anyone would ever work in religion." Don't miss the full picture. Here is a guy who stands over sewer systems ten-hours a day, holding a hose, pumping sludge. And he can't understand why anyone would want to be a pastor.

I've thought about my septic man over the years and I have come to see his point. Shepherding is about leading people who don't want to be led. It is about becoming the scum of the earth for the sake of the Gospel.

Shepherding is about faithfulness, not popularity. Beware of popularity. Amy Carmichael, in her book Gold Cord, the story of the Dohnavur Fellowship ministry in India said this: "The work was to develop upon lines that would not find general acceptance, and we had to learn the unchangeable truth: Our Master has never promised success. He demands obedience. He expects faithfulness. Results are His concern, not ours. And our reputation is a matter of no consequence at all."

Why lead?

After Jesus made breakfast for the disciples by the Sea of Tiberius, he asked Peter to go for a walk. After walking a short distance, Jesus stopped, turned to Simon Peter and pointed back to the other disciples. "Simon, son of John," Jesus asked, " do you truly love me more than these?"

"Yes, Lord," he said, "you know that I love you." Jesus said, "Feed my lambs."

Again Jesus said, "Simon son of John, do you truly love me?" He answered, "Yes, Lord, you know that I love you."

Jesus said, "Take care of my sheep."

The third time he said to him, "Simon, son of John, do you love me?" Peter was hurt because Jesus asked him the third time, "Do you love me?" He said, "Lord, you know all things; you know that I love you." Jesus said, "Feed my sheep."

Shepherding the church springs from loving God.

The motivation for leadership is the same for every other call and every other action – to love the Lord your God with all your heart, soul and strength. A shepherd must love God so much that bearing curses and persecution for His sake is considered a badge of honor: "They were stoned; they were sawed in two; they were put to death by the sword. They went about in sheepskins and goatskins, destitute, persecuted and mistreated– the world was not worthy of them." (Heb. 11:36,37)

The evangelist Billy Kim once told a story of American tourists visiting a leper colony in India. One tourist, upon seeing an American missionary woman cleaning the sores of a leper, remarked, "I would not do that for a million dollars." The missionary looked up at the man and replied, "I would not either."

It is for the love of God and no other benefit or reason that we are called. Such love binds wounds, loves the unlovely and suffers with and for the sake of others. The motivation for shepherding people cannot be reputation or financial gain. Only love.

Peter instructs leaders to shepherd God's flock "not because you must, but because you are willing, as God wants you to be; not greedy for money, but eager to serve." I wonder what was on Peter's mind when the Holy Spirit directed him to write this? Do you suppose he was recalling Jesus words to him?

Again Jesus said, "Simon, son of John, do you truly love me?" He answered, "Yes, Lord, you know that I love you." Jesus said, "Take care of my sheep." (John 21:16) Jesus told Peter to "take care of my sheep." Jesus knew that by caring for sheep Peter would be loving his Savior.

To summarize all that Scripture teaches about the role of shepherd-leader is this: Lead in Love.

Ultimately, the purpose of leading the flock of God is not saving people, not serving God, not doing good things, but loving God.

At the end of John's Gospel, just after the story of Jesus telling Peter to feed the sheep, John gives a telling insight into Peter, an insight for each one who God calls to shepherd people. Peter turned and saw that the disciple whom Jesus loved was following them. . . When Peter saw him, he asked, "Lord, what about him?" Jesus answered, "If I want him to remain alive until I return, what is that to you? You must follow me." (John 21:20-22)

Leadership, in the final analysis, is not about a call or a spiritual gift or power or building a church or helping the poor and weak. Leadership is about a deep, abiding passion for God. It is about love. It is about following Christ.

The gift of leadership is a gift of, and participation in, grace. But even the most gifted leader in the world, as 1 Corinthians 13 reminds us, cannot lead without love. Without love, leadership is void of Christ, and anything without Christ is nothing.

The shepherd leader leads in love.

Epilogue

May the God of peace, who through the blood of the eternal covenant
brought back from the dead our Lord Jesus, that great Shepherd of the
sheep, equip you with everything good for doing his will, and may he
work in us what is pleasing to him, through Jesus Christ, to whom
be glory for ever and ever. Amen. Hebrews 13: 20,21

We began this narrative with a story about my ewe Elizabeth and the triplets we lost one early winter morning. But the tale does not end there. . .

After I knew the triplets had died, I called my neighbor to tell him what happened. Jed informed me that, strangely, one of his ewes also had triplets just the day before. In fact, the lambs were in trouble because the ewe did not have enough milk for even two, let alone three lambs.

Suddenly it occurred to us that Elizabeth might help. Perhaps Elizabeth could adopt two of Jed's lambs.

I led Elizabeth down to Jed's barn and into a lambing pen to try to graft his two lambs to my ewe. Elizabeth's lambs had never nursed so I unplugged her teats to get her milk flowing (just like milking a cow) smearing some of the milk on the backs of each lamb.

Sheep identify their young by smelling their rear end. They will only accept a lamb that has their distinct scent which is carried in their milk. Once a lamb nurses from the mother, the lamb will only be accepted by that ewe because of the scent. Their own mother will not recognize them as her own.

By taking milk from Elizabeth and spreading it on the lambs, we hoped to "graft" these lambs to Elizabeth. Then we waited. After about two hours it was clear she had accepted the lambs as her own.

Elizabeth stayed in Jed's barn for the next three months nurturing her "born again" lambs.